THE SUCCESS PLAYBOOK

Printed in the United States of America.
First Printing, 2016

ISBN    978-0-9973045-0-3
ISBN    978-0-9973045-1-0

1. SEL027000 SELF-HELP / Personal Growth / Success
2. SEL045000 SELF-HELP / Journaling

Think Bold, Be Bold Media
P.O. Box 1206
Fairview, OR  97024

www.ChristopherCumby.com

## PRINCIPLES AND STRATEGIES FOR BUILDING A RICH AND HAPPY LIFE

# Christopher Cumby

# CONTENTS

Dear Reader,

Personal development is a topic I deeply care about. Following great leaders of the past and brilliant minds of the present, I have studied the natural laws of success over the last two decades. Though the journey to optimum self–development is a personal one, it is also universal – remarkable results are available to those who invest their energy into bettering themselves. We all have the opportunity to become the most successful versions of ourselves if we simply examine the lessons before us and trust in our ability to follow them.

In preparation for this journey, let us first define success and really understand the playbook concept:

Success is the attainment of wealth, position, honors, or the like.

Playbook is a book containing the scripts of one or more plays or strategic moves.

*The Success Playbook: Principles and Strategies to Help You Build a Rich and Happy Life* is your personal guide outlining strategic moves for the attainment of your success.

You will ultimately design your own success playbook, define your own success, and be coached on how to achieve it. You will learn, and apply, the basic fundamentals of success through time–tested practices. Your journal will be your number one tool for success.

This book allows you to master your habits, discover your genius zone, and learn how to make accurate decisions, manifesting in precise results. You'll discover the keys to happy living and getting exactly what you want in life. You will learn to self–assess, and expand your knowledge as you acquire new techniques and behaviors. Your foundation of knowledge is your most important asset as you reach for your dreams. Building a STRONG foundation enables you to build HIGHER. I will teach you to master this concept and create the rock–solid base to your future.

Each chapter in this book is outlined to be simple and clear. You'll learn to apply the four basic pillars that create the foundation for success. You will have the Playbook in your hands so you can quickly and easily master the rules of success before you even play the game. By following the rules of this game and combining them with appropriate actions and steadfast determination, you will achieve the success of your dreams.

It's time to build your own success journey. We all play this game of life – together we can all succeed, achieve, and accomplish.

Do what you love, turn faith into action and find the courage to try.


Sincerely,

Christopher Cumby

www.ChristopherCumby.com

# Getting Started

## Building the Foundation:
## Introducing the Pillars That Support Your Success

> *"Hard work, dedication to the job at hand,*
> *and the determination that whether we win or lose,*
> *we have applied the best of ourselves to the task at hand."*
>
> Vince Lombardi

*Success.*

*Success is much more than what you have. It's also how you respond when you no longer have it.*

*Success takes great resiliency, grit, and determination.*

*We all have it within reach.*

Most people aspire to achieve some level of success. Of course what you may define as success may be completely insignificant to the person standing next to you. Be it a promotion, a new car, a larger house, a happy family – we all view success as something specific to our own lives.

The great thing about success – and what makes it so entirely special – is that we each have the exciting opportunity and responsibility to decide how we define it. We are the ones who determine how exactly it manifests in our lives.

Regardless of how you define it, the fundamentals are the same. To prepare yourself for the journey to your personal success, you must accept two essential points:

1. You must be willing to change.
2. You must be willing to open your mind and learn.

Your playbook is a contract, of sorts, propelling you forward in the direction of change. It is a place to write down your thoughts, your goals, your desires, even your shortcomings, as you track your personal growth. Documenting aspirations, setting goals and monitoring growth will hold you accountable.

Just as any building requires a solid foundation to be strong, success requires strong desires, positive thought, definitive purpose, and inspired action to create a life of abundance. Yet many people don't know what they want or don't make decisions that work in favor of their true self. You are what you think about, so think positively and with purpose.

How do you build a strong foundation for your life? First, identify what you don't want. Identify the things in your life that are not positive or bringing you down. Take an honest assessment of your current situation, accept it, and then shift your focus to what you *do* want.

Success is very much like a house: with a strong foundation, you can construct the home of your dreams. Lay the proper groundwork and anything is possible. The same is possible in your quest for success. The four pillars outlined in this book will serve as your foundation, giving you the necessary support as you build a life of abundance. You will use them every day. They will become an intuitive part of your thought process. They'll influence how you think, how you conduct yourself in the world and they'll guide you along your path to success.

Once mastered, these pillars will provide you with an amazing skill set that differentiates you from so many others. Preparing yourself for this step requires the rewiring of your mind to accept only positive messages. Throughout the book, I have included digital meditations to help prepare you for this new chapter in positive thinking. I also recommend finding a journal where you can freely document your thoughts and focus your attention on the goals ahead. These two practices are essential in finding your success.

## The Four Pillars

These are the basics, the support for everything else to come. This foundation is your most important asset as you go after your dreams. *Building a STRONG foundation enables you to build HIGHER.*

### Pillar #1: Be Careful Whom You Listen to

Always seek facts, not just opinions. The number one reason people give up on their dreams: they listen to the wrong people. There are so many differing opinions in this world, but you have to make the conscious choice to listen to supportive and encouraging opinions. Ultimately, you will learn to trust yourself and your intuition.

### Pillar #2: Keep Learning

You don't know what you don't know. A basic requirement of success is continuous learning. Being a student of life will fuel your growth because without growth, your dreams will lie stagnant and begin to fade.

### Pillar #3: Accept Change

If you want change in your life, you must first be the change. Life *is* change, and your ability to adapt and accept that will allow you to enjoy life more. Be fluid, be flexible and let that "flow" lead you to exactly where you want to go. As Bruce Lee said:

> "You must be shapeless, formless, like water. When you pour water in a cup, it becomes the cup. When you pour water in a bottle...it becomes the bottle. When you pour water in a teapot...it becomes the teapot. Water can drip and it can crash ... Become like water, my friend."

## Pillar #4: Know Why You Want Something

Make sure you know *why* you want something in your life, and focus on it. Knowing your *why* is more powerful than knowing exactly how you will achieve it. When you believe in your desires and take logical steps toward them each day, the universal laws of attraction will provide the path that is required for you to get there.

## Putting It Together

Years ago, as I was struggling with a particular business, I started learning and applying success basics to my own life. I was intrigued, and curious, looking inward because I felt it my responsibility to better my life. These simple, initial steps began my journey to a more meaningful, organized, and successful life.

With an honest eye, I acknowledged and accepted the things I didn't like about my life. Then I turned my attention to my happiness factors – my family, my friends and my passions. And what do we all want at the end of the day? To do more of what makes us happy! I realized that to experience more of what makes me happy, I needed more time. Turning my attention to what I loved inspired my drive to create the life I wanted.

At that point I realized, I had no idea where to start! So I sought out people who were doing what I enjoyed doing and started asking questions. How were they doing it? What steps were they taking to reach their goals? Could I emulate them and achieve my own success?

These influential, inspiring people had several common strategies that contributed to their success. They embrace the four pillars and put them to use every day in every aspect of their lives. Another unifying trait? These leaders embraced positivity and realized what a powerful influencer it was on a person's energy, outlook and determination. I learned that believing in yourself, your actions, your outcomes – it is the most powerful first step that anyone can take. As the old saying goes: whether you believe you can or you can't, you're right!

6

Finding the courage to take that first step in turning your passions into reality can be intimidating. However, I knew that if I could achieve my own success, if I could finally live the life that I have dreamed of living, then I would help others do the same. The knowledge I acquired, the steps I took to reach my goals, I wanted to share this so I could give you the inspiration and motivation to go after what you really want, demolish the fears that keep you back, climb to a new level of accurate thinking.

This was the inspiration for my own playbook. Yours may look substantially different from mine but the principles, foundation, and pillars may still be similar. Completing my own playbook was exciting, but that excitement pales in comparison to the gratitude I feel in playing a role in helping you create yours.

To help you along the path of achieving your own success, **this** *Success Playbook* will become **your** *Success Playbook*. Each chapter includes a Playbook Exercise and a Success Meditation, both designed to explore and reinforce the lessons we learn throughout the book. They will give you both practical and reflective practice of applying the lessons to achieving success to your own life.

Remember, success is a journey, but it is one that we will take together. It is a journey that can be navigated with substantially less difficulty with a sound game plan and a set of resources to make the journey not only a prosperous one, but also an exciting one.

## Playbook Exercise: Getting Started

In your journal, write a letter to yourself and date it one year from today. Write about how your life has changed in the past year and be descriptive. Think about every dream, goal, and aspiration you have and write them down as if you have achieved each one within this past year. *Be sure to write in the present tense* – only using words like "I have" and "I am" and not "I will" or "I want."

Be creative. In your letter, you can include the actions you took to reach these milestones or the feelings and emotions that came with realizing these goals. Be detailed. If travel is one of your aspirations, write about the spectacular sights on one of your many adventures!

This exercise is designed to show you the power of positive thinking, visualization and accountability by writing down your wildest dreams as though they have already come true. The power of positivity goes a long way, and your ability to believe in yourself will guide you to the life you dream of living.

**TIP** – Write like you are updating a close friend on your greatest successes of the past year. Be imaginative and have FUN!

## Success Meditation:
## Getting Started – Connecting With Your Inner–Self

Visit the following link to access the digital downloads for each chapter's Success Meditations:

www.ChristopherCumby.com/SuccessMeditation

**JOURNAL NOTES:**

_____

_____

_____

_____

_____

_____

_____

_____

_____

_____

_____

_____

_____

_____

_____

_____

**JOURNAL NOTES:**

_____

_____

_____

_____

_____

_____

_____

_____

_____

_____

_____

_____

_____

_____

_____

_____

_____

_____

_____

# 1     The First Pillar: Be Careful Who You Listen To

> *"The mind is not a vessel to be filled,*
> *but a fire to be kindled."*
>
> Plutarch

Applying the four pillars of success will ignite a fire within your heart and soul. Let it burn bright! That fire will warm your mind and light your way – you need only open ears and an accessible mind to be on your way.

Often, those around you act as elevators. Getting on the right elevator, or surrounding yourself with the right people, will raise your spirits, your motivation level, and your desire to do your best. Paying attention to negative opinions from pessimistic people, you'll quickly find yourself on the elevator that takes you directly to the basement. We all start on the ground floor, but what we do prior to stepping foot on that elevator often dictates which direction we'll take.

## Always Seek Facts over Mere Opinions

Beginning my journey, I didn't know what I didn't know. Simply put, life has a lot to teach us and the learning curve is steep. Understanding that we all begin as vessels, and that it takes time to fill these vessels, is the first step toward a prosperous journey through life.

Let's be honest: have you ever found yourself in a conversation nodding along in agreement simply because you felt alone in being out of the loop? There is no shame in not knowing! There is even less shame in acknowledging that we lack experience. Why? Because identifying what you need to develop is, in fact, a development. Understand that you have questions to ask and you are not the first, nor the last, to wonder about the same topic.

Remember: there are endless opportunities waiting once you accept that you don't know it all. From there, you will be on your way to knowing more than you know.

The search for facts is where it all begins. Everyone has opinions. Just walk down the street and people will offer you plenty of opinions, whether you asked for them or not! But facts are harder to find. They hide from you. They are the fruits of the journey, the bounty from the adventure. The ability to create requires knowledge, and the number one reason people don't achieve their dreams (or even go after their dreams) is that *they listen to the wrong people.* Opinions are a dime a dozen, let's focus on knowing when to listen and when to put on your proverbial earmuffs. Knowledge is power, and gaining accurate knowledge will get you to your goals much faster.

> "The great enemy of truth is very often not the lie – deliberate, contrived and dishonest – but the myth – persistent, persuasive and unrealistic. Too often we hold fast to the clichés of our forebears. We subject all facts to a prefabricated set of interpretations. We enjoy the comfort of opinion without the discomfort of thought."
>
> John F. Kennedy

As you set sail on the voyage toward your goals, focus on your destination and keep your eyes open along the way. Catching the wrong wind will force you to alter your course or risk ending up at an unexpected destination. Misinformation is everywhere, be able to discern it. Sometimes the difference between a fact and an opinion may seem small, but the distinction in your results can be substantial. Classify facts into important and relevant vs. non–important and irrelevant to ensure you reach your main objectives. Within these small clarifications, greatness is born.

## Listen to Yourself First

Many times I have been asked, "Who do you listen to?" My answer is always the same: "You must first learn to listen to your gut instinct, then find people who align with that direction and listen to them."

This is a skill you'll understand and agree with rather quickly but as with any skill, it requires practice and persistence to get better at it. As you gain confidence, you'll find yourself better able to listen to yourself first. When confidence is built, it can withstand many challenges that you have yet to face. However, when they do occur, you will be armed with a powerful skill to solve them quickly. [*No one in this world cares for you more than you do. No one knows you better than you do.*] *No one understands what you need and how you need it better than you do.* So why would you listen to anyone else before listening to yourself?

So often we allow the mere opinions of others to impact and completely sway our own beliefs. We allow the noise around us to affect how we view ourselves. Even when the facts support a different conclusion, we remain affected by opinions rarely based in truth. It is natural, *but it is harmful.* Because we take much of our self–worth from the thoughts and feelings of others, we position ourselves to be at the mercy of others.

Take a moment and look around. Consider those people around you and understand that these people, and their morals, opinions, and interactions with you, have an integral effect on your life. But only if you allow them to. Listen to yourself first, and then let everyone else support what you already believe.

[Be prudent enough to surround yourself with people who *have what you want and have been where you are.*] These two statements are crucial to the development of your success. When you align yourself with qualified mentors, you'll begin to see significant shifts in your life. Mentoring is critical for the attainment of success, as no one has ever reached any significant success without the aid of others.

Having mentors will help you see your blind spots, guide you in the right direction, and ultimately provide you with honest information to drive you toward your aspirations. Mentorship can come in so many different ways; you may have someone at your company you look up to and can meet with regularly or you may want to emulate an international business mogul so you subscribe to their YouTube channel and read all their books. You only need to figure out which method works best for you. Pick the mentors and methods that best fit your lifestyle best and run with them!

**Audio:** Listen to CDs, MP3s, audio books, podcasts, etc. They're very economical, many are free to download or stream, and you can maximize your time by listening to them on your commute, during your workout, or while you work.

**Reading:** This method is the most popular and easiest to access. You can review the content again and again and make personal notes to yourself. Books and blogs are two of the best resources for this purpose.

**One–on–One Mentoring:** This approach is very powerful and is usually done in person or via the telephone.

**Seminars:** This is an incredibly effective way to access exclusive information and see your mentor up close and personal. Most seminar attendees, regardless of topic or speaker, will walk away more energized, positive and confident about the direction they are heading.

**Video:** Have you watched TED talks or YouTube videos on subjects you find interesting? Video is one of the most popular ways of disseminating information today. Take the time to see what's out there!

No matter the medium, make it a point to *listen carefully and take notes in your playbook*, so you always have the opportunity to return to that moment in time by reviewing your material.

Emulating people you admire gives you proof of the potential success you can accomplish. The fact that these mentors accomplished their goals and attained their desires is proof that nurturing and growing your own beliefs will yield the same results. But who you surround yourself with, and who you listen to, can wholly determine whether you succeed or not – so don't listen to the wrong people! Once you choose your preferred medium, write down exactly what you want to learn from your mentors and keep this in a place you can go back and refer to frequently.

## Facts Drive Success, Opinions Kill Dreams

Once you choose to *whom* you'll listen, focus on *how* you'll listen. My advice is to always listen twice: once to the provided *information*, and then to *who* is providing the information. As an entrepreneur, I have found this instrumental in guiding my success and avoiding missteps. Call it a double–filtration system to ensure the information you receive is clear and transparent.

Will you be challenged along this path? Absolutely, but you will overcome it. I have shared my dreams and goals with negative people whose only response was pessimism. When launching my first business, I was told I would be happier and safer in an environment that was stable and recession proof. I didn't listen and forged ahead. I researched and found mentors in my field of interest. Within two years, my new business venture had generated millions of dollars and I easily surpassed my previous financial package. If I had just stayed put, allowing the negative talkers to influence my decision, I would have missed out on the happiness, opportunity and financial success of my new venture.

When you find yourself in this situation, and you will, ask yourself if the person before you is providing constructive criticism or just saying "no" to your ideas. Stay firm in your beliefs and acknowledge that this damaging feedback holds no power over you. Negativity will kill your dreams and stifle your goals. Opinions are always going to be there, but you must learn to filter them effectively.

Playing it safe doesn't do you any favors; it doesn't push you to be better personally or professionally, it celebrates mediocrity. And you are not mediocre. We are all capable of achieving more, so engage your mentor and be careful whom you listen to. Having the right mentors will give you direction, but you'll want a strong support system to help you execute your directives.

## Turning Down the Noise: Building Your Dream Team

Surrounding yourself with a dream team of like–minded individuals that support and encourage you is crucial to your success; no matter what path you want to take. But how exactly do you build a dream team? Who do you choose? What do you do first?

Google changed the world as we know it, and it all started with a small dream team, a powerful mastermind created between Larry Page and Sergey Brin in the mid–nineties. Google is an odd name, it has no meaning, yet that word has become synonymous with surfing the web. Google has become a verb and before 1996 it didn't even exist. Both Larry and Sergey met at Stanford University while pursuing PhDs in computer science. Larry was already working on a research paper for a project called "backrub," and Sergey joined his mastermind to author a research paper focusing on a large–scale search engine that would eventually become the PageRank algorithm. Having two minds converge on the idea broke down the complexity and scale of the project, and together both Larry and Sergey made history.

What Larry and Sergey may not have realized at the time is that they had just entered into one of the most powerful masterminds ever created. This harmonious blending of two minds created a third mind, the culmination of their own, which went on to discover and create one of technology's most powerful tools. Unwittingly, they created one of the greatest dream teams in the history of the world.

Google is just one example of a dream team, but there are many more. Virgin Group owes its success to founder Sir Richard Branson and his partnership with Nik Powell, who formed an alliance with

Branson in 1972. When Virgin Records was sold to EMI Music, in a very lucrative deal, it gave Branson and Powell the freedom to focus their creative energies on more innovative projects. Virgin Group's offerings went from music publishing to space travel, opening everyone's minds to the infinite possibilities available to those of us who believe we can.

It is documented throughout history that the use of a dream team, or mastermind, is the way to exponentially multiply your potential outcome. One of my silent mentors, Peter Diamandis, points out the concept of a dream team in a recent blog post about his book *Bold: How to Go Big, Create Wealth and Impact the World.*

Peter says:

> "Small teams, authority and autonomy, trust between all players, a simple plan with high flexibility to make changes on the fly, isolation from the outside, and early testing."

This is how to create a powerful mastermind.

Peter goes on to quote psychologist Garry Latham, *"You have to believe in what you're doing. Big goals work best when there's an alignment between an individual's values and the desired outcome of the goal. When everything lines up, we're totally committed — meaning we're paying even more attention, are even more resilient, and are way more productive as a result."*

When I decided to leave my comfortable job and go out on my own, I partnered with three other people. Armed with a common goal, our minds harmonized on the outcome we desired and we not only met our goals, we exceeded them. This was my first meaningful mastermind and creation of a dream team. Since those days I have created dream teams for everything I endeavor on. They may be in the form of silent mentors, imaginary council (we will explore this topic later in the book), or real–life people. Regardless, this essential support positioned me to achieve so much more than I could have on my own.

As you develop and grow, the noise around you will often get louder. It just comes with the territory. You, and only you, get to decide exactly who and what you want to listen to. Develop the crucial skills to filter out those who offer little and exchange them for those who can offer lots: lots of support, lots of experience, lots of feedback, and lots of positivity.

Listen to yourself and do your own thinking. It is your gut, your mind, your heart, and your soul that will always act as the guiding light for your success and your goals.

### Playbook Exercise 1:

Take a moment to answer these integral questions and write down the answers in a journal.

- Who will you choose as mentors?
- What would you like to learn from them?
- What method will you employ to gain that knowledge?
- What does your dream team look like?
- How will these people help you improve your current position?

This will be the first step in acknowledging your goals and setting clear parameters about how you'll achieve them.

### Success Meditation #1 – Harmonization

www.ChristopherCumby.com/SuccessMeditation

**JOURNAL NOTES:**

**JOURNAL NOTES:**

_____

_____

_____

_____

_____

_____

_____

_____

_____

_____

_____

_____

_____

_____

_____

_____

_____

# 2 The Second Pillar: Keep Learning

> *"The years teach much which the days never know."*
>
> Ralph Waldo Emerson

A wealth of knowledge is available to each of us in our respective journeys, but the responsibility is ours alone to find this information, assess it and use it for our own betterment. Because if we don't educate ourselves, who will? This particular pillar gets easier with repetition, and before long your evaluation of opportunities and challenges will be completely ingrained.

Let's start the journey with the second pillar by first discussing how we learn new things. There are four steps to learning:

1. Unconscious incompetence
2. Conscious incompetence
3. Conscious competence
4. Unconscious competence

The reality is that we are first *unconscious* and *incompetent*, unaware of exactly how to reach our goals. Meaning, *we don't know what we don't know*. We see a destination, we understand there will be a journey, but what transpires between those two dots is truly an unknown.

Think back to your biology class. Remember halfway through the course when your teacher put a dead frog in front of you and your classmates? You wouldn't know how to dissect a frog if you weren't otherwise required to do so. Still, there you were, scalpel in hand, prior to taking that class, dissecting a frog, and how to do so, likely never even crossed your mind. That unconsciousness, or not knowing what you didn't know, would have kept you in the dark.

But through that exercise in biology you received a wealth of knowledge you wouldn't otherwise possess. Learning is critical to your success. And that learning starts with discovery, or beginning the process of discovering what isn't already clear and apparent.

The second stage of learning is *conscious incompetence*. This is the realization that something exists, but you are still unaware of how it works or why it exists. This is where you begin to understand your surroundings and question why things function the way they do. You just know the basics, similar to initially meeting an acquaintance. Learning starts as your attention is directed to the process of understanding something. This is the first step of *knowing what you don't know*.

The third stage of learning is *conscious competence*, or the stage of application. This is the point where you start *knowing what you need to know*. The application of knowledge is the action of attaining what you seek. This is commonly the place where you manifest a mastermind and engage mentors to help you on your journey.

The fourth and final stage of learning is *unconscious competence*, and in this stage your mind clicks into automatic response. This is where your habits take over and play a more important, intuitive role in your life. When we are operating in unconscious competence, our vibrational frequencies mimic our feelings and emotions. You can think of vibrational frequencies as the good or bad energy you sense about a person; they are determined by the dominant thoughts and beliefs you hold in your consciousness. Our connection to our gut instinct, or intuitive mind, starts to form here. Learning to trust this process takes time and effort until it becomes part of your hypnotic awareness. These habitual responses are reactionary and are the pinnacle of your learning process; this acquired knowledge becomes second nature.

The economic crash of 2008 crippled America's economy and its housing market. Some of the largest companies in the banking and mortgage industries were rocked, resulting in a record–breaking number of home foreclosures in the U.S. Why did this occur? Could it have been the result of listening to the wrong people and not knowing what we don't know?

We do know that these industries failed to outline all the facts. People trusted them, failing to seek out those relevant facts. As a result, this crisis had a global impact that very few were prepared to face. Not only did this have an effect on millions of Americans, the fallout impacted countries around the world that depended on the strength of the U.S. economy. Were the two success pillars followed? Not likely.

Years later, we are still using terms like "recovery" and "on the mend" when discussing the strength of the U.S. economy. Why? Because we *now know what we know* about how and why this economic crash happened. Unfortunately, too many people learned this lesson the hard way. A blind reliance on institutionalized beliefs is dangerous. Armed now with the understanding of the first two pillars, you are an objective listener and follow your instincts. You will not blindly follow the masses, but rather educate yourself and learn how to discern and assimilate facts. Our temporary failures in life hold the seeds of success for our future; consciously learning from these otherwise difficult lessons can ensure they don't happen again. Look for these seeds within your own stories; they are hidden opportunities to be seized.

Is it important to continue *learning* in your life? Learning can mitigate much despair, and I highly recommend focusing your attention on always being a student and always being *teachable*!

## Stay Teachable

Remaining teachable is a basic requirement of success. Refusing to learn the lessons life gives us will prevent personal growth. If you are not growing, your dreams will die. So let's begin this section by explaining this important concept and then outlining the steps needed to advance your continuous curiosity.

In my youth, school never excited me. I didn't see the point of learning things that I wasn't interested in and was fairly certain I would never use later in life. As I matured, my outlook changed. I realized the importance of education – both conventional and self–taught – and how my thirst for knowledge would influence my life's work. Education is a crucial aspect of success. It provides a wide lens through which to look at life, and it opens the doors of substantial opportunity in both our personal and professional endeavors.

> "Take the attitude of a student, never be too big to ask questions, never know too much to learn something new."
>
> Og Mandino

This all begins by being teachable. You will never have the opportunity to learn if you are not teachable. The simplest way to gauge our level of, and commitment to, our eagerness to learn is by identifying how much we are willing to sacrifice. If you really want to achieve something great, you must be willing to give up something, at least initially, in order to obtain it. You may find yourself trading time, money, instant gratification, social outings or just sleeping in so you can obtain something far more coveted and valuable down the road.

**Share It All**

What are the things you do every day that drive your desire to be in constant learning mode? Identify them, and then share them. Let me share some of my strategies for being a student of life.

Be an avid reader. Books provoke creative thinking, identify blind spots, and allow the exploration of new interests. I found that reading a topic or passage that really excited me, or left me with more questions than answers, would compel me to learn more in order to gain a deeper understanding of the concept. This cultivates a need to always want more – question what is in front of you and never settle for not knowing the answer.

Asking more detailed questions is another way to actively seek information because better questions result in better answers. Become a better researcher and surround yourself with people who are smarter than you. It is an important step in building a dream team and formulating your mastermind.

I also have a unique routine I use when faced with opportunities or challenges: I put it to my silent imaginary council.

*What is a silent imaginary council?*

Well, my silent imaginary council consists of the following people: Walt Disney, Mahatma Gandhi, Abraham Lincoln, Ralph Waldo Emerson, Earl Nightingale, Napoleon Hill, Oprah Winfrey, Zig Ziglar, Brian Tracy, Albert Einstein, Jesus Christ, Bob Proctor and Peter Diamandis. This council is a corkboard with a picture of each of these people mentioned above. I routinely use a meditative process to quiet my mind and connect with these people as if they were in the room with me. I ask them questions in my mind, and based on each person's personality I get different perspectives and answers that help me to make decisions.

*So how did I choose my silent council?*

Each person on my council has a quality that I admire, that resonates deeply with me. What they stand for mirrors what I want for myself. The same can be true for you. Take the time to create a silent council, choose people you believe can be difference–makers in your life. After doing so, rely upon them for direction, for guidance, and for direct and unfiltered opinions.

My silent council developed as I transitioned from a very lucrative career to launching my first business. I was called crazy for leaving a six–figure job to go into business for myself. Once I made the decision to pursue my dream, I took action. I heavily researched the industry I was entering, weighed the risks and rewards associated with it, asked detailed questions of those around me and "consulted" with my newly created silent council. In these actions, I looked for evidence and reinforcement to support my decision. I went with my gut and found the positive support I needed to move forward.

Taking a moment out of your day to reflect on an influential, silent mentor's viewpoint can really put things into perspective for you. It's similar to asking yourself, "What would Mom or Dad say?" when faced with a dilemma – except now you get multiple perspectives and your decision probably won't get you grounded.

## The Greatest Students of Our Time

Focusing on the second pillar of the *Success Playbook*, you don't know what you don't know, culminates in the desire to be a student – to learn hard, embrace opportunity, and listen to those who came before you. Try listening to your silent council; let their wealth of knowledge be a guiding force in your life. Aim high in your selection. Choose a council of extraordinary students of life; let their contributions to the world motivate you.

*How did they do it?*

Walt Disney, the man behind "The Happiest Place on Earth," never stopped learning. He began his career as a cartoonist, before starting The Walt Disney Company with his brother Roy. Walt, a gifted artist, pioneered the age of animation. He was constantly a student of his art, mastering still art to moving animation to theme parks.

Steve Jobs is credited with transforming technology as we know it. He wasn't content with the status quo; his curiosity led him to seek solutions that revolutionized the world. He built a dream team of intelligent, progressive thinkers and encouraged their candid feedback. Jobs understood the importance of continuous education and humbly believed in surrounding yourself with smarter people to make your team stronger.

How about Albert Einstein?

His theories changed how we see the world. Personally, he continues to inspire me through one singular statement:

> ## "Nothing happens until something moves."

This saying is a constant reminder to keep moving, stay active and not fall into the trap of procrastination or inaction. Einstein was the ultimate student, imaginatively pursuing solutions, remaining unsatisfied until he received his coveted answers.

The road to success for these innovators was not without opposition or adversity. Like many of us, they faced temporary defeats yet overcame them. I salute them, and I salute all people who find the strength to rise above their current situation and see the greatness that is possible. Education is opportunity in its simplest form – and it is opportunity that teaches you the most important lessons.

### Choosing a Mentor

Almost every success story has a mentor or guiding force helping the successful person through adversity and obstacles. So how do you choose your silent council, and how can you access their knowledge? Your life is a reflection of the people with whom you surround yourself. Now is the time to start choosing your greatest assets, allies, and mentors.

Growing up, I was a paperboy. That job taught me a very useful lesson that has stayed with me throughout my life. A more experienced colleague shared that the best way to get tips was to memorize all my customers' names and remember little things about them. He recommended I buy a journal and write these important details down.

The concept of journaling is one I completely embrace and use daily. In fact, I have stacks of notepads from over the years. My whole entrepreneurial life has been well documented! It was through that mentorship (even though I didn't recognize it at the time) that I learned my first valuable life lesson. The same can be true for you.

Write out words that inspire you in your journal. Take five minutes and find words you have a strong affection for – words that make you feel good when you write them down. Build a list of inspiring words, use words associated with each of your silent council and you'll be well on your way to building your mastermind of great mentors.

Here are some guidelines for selecting and organizing people to follow and learn from:

- Find people who help you see your blind spots and will provide feedback. Their guidance should come from experience you want or need. Choose people you believe in and trust, people who believe in you, and people who have something you can believe in for yourself.

- Choose people who have blazed the paths that you hope to journey. Following in the footsteps of those who came before you can offer tried and true tactics to reach your goals.

- Don't hesitate to expand or reduce your mentors or silent council. As your vision changes, so should the people who support your vision. There is no perfect equation; continually reevaluate and reassess those people on your team.

- Be willing to learn. You don't know what you don't know. The only way to bridge that gap and identify the lessons you don't know is by remaining a student of life.

I always knew I would take the road less traveled. Although exciting and terrifying, I found my way with the help of my mentors and silent council. You will find your mentors, and as you build a stronger intuition, you will know which ones are right for you.

The second pillar of the *Success Playbook* is *you don't know what you don't know*. Accepting this concept will reduce what you don't know. It will take time, energy, and effort, but that nominal investment will be repaid in full when you find yourself not just surviving major challenges, but succeeding at them.

Commit to expanding your education and be disciplined in your approach. Make sure the knowledge you seek is sound and its source is legitimate. Embrace the big changes that come with this shift, focus on the positive and be open to the new opportunities that await you.

**Playbook Exercise 2:**

Map out the financial and scheduling "budget" of your personal commitments and find the resources you need to get to the next step.

1. Write a list of the personal activities you enjoy.

2. Detail the weekly time/financial/commitment of each one.

3. Write down the new activity that you plan to add to your week and determine the financial or time commitments this new endeavor will require.

4. Balance your budget! What can you defer, for the time being, to get you closer to your dreams?

What are you willing to trade for the opportunity of a lifetime?


**Success Meditation #2: – Connecting With Success**

www.ChristopherCumby.com/SuccessMeditation

**JOURNAL NOTES:**

**JOURNAL NOTES:**

_____

_____

_____

_____

_____

_____

_____

_____

_____

_____

_____

_____

_____

_____

_____

_____

_____

_____

# 3  The Third Pillar: Accept Change

> *"You must be the change you wish to see in the world."*
>
> Mahatma Gandhi

In reality, we all have an enormous responsibility, even a duty, to work together to create and manifest the best life imaginable. Humanity relies upon each of us to play our respective roles and move the needle in the direction of a collective heartbeat. Oftentimes we forget that we are each an example to so many people: our friends, our family, and our colleagues. They look to us for guidance, education, and acceptance. At times, they may look to us to help them manage difficult times and influence the way they live. For that reason, we all have a responsibility to "be the change to see the change."

We have an exciting opportunity to lead by example, and this chapter will show you how. Up to this point, we have learned the importance of the first two pillars:

1. *Be Careful Who You Listen To*
2. *You Don't Know What You Don't Know*

Let's now turn our attention to the next pillar: *Be the change to see the change.* On a personal level, this particular pillar offers a great deal of guidance and is a mantra by which to live life.

Recall the Bruce Lee quote I mentioned earlier, *"You must be shapeless, formless, like water . . . Become like water, my friend."* When I first read this quote, it sang to me and influenced me, changing how I looked at everything in life. I practice this concept of being like water every day, and I feel the impact of its promise with quietude and calmness.

By definition, change means: "to make or become different." What does that mean to you? Being different is what makes us all unique; no one person has lived the same life. So being different is a natural state – one that should be embraced, celebrated, and then used as a way to distinguish yourself and your journey.

I first discovered the power of change during a transitional chapter in my life. Dire straits, really. I was almost broke and soon to be homeless if I didn't make something happen fast. I felt as if I was on a runaway train, heading straight for a cliff and unable to slow down. I soon realized that I had to be the change I wanted to see in my life. If not me, then who? I had no choice but to make it happen on my own terms.

So I made some very specific decisions about how to change the direction of my life.

I believed I could do it. I wrote down my plan of action. Then I did it. And once I did that, I knew that I could help others follow my path. The only unknown is it. You get to decide what it is that you want; the result is up to you.

Committing to change is …well, a commitment. When I began one of my companies, its primary concentration was strategic sales consulting. When a new opportunity arose, I recognized its potential and knew the company had to change to be successful in this new space. Following the first two pillars, I shifted the company's focus to brokering energy. I never anticipated such a drastic change, but I listened when opportunity knocked. I opened that door and it was obvious what an exciting prospect stood before me!

That was years ago, and the company has transitioned again to a strategic sales firm helping CEOs and entrepreneurs grow their businesses. I've witnessed first hand that it's necessary to be fluid and change with the times. Being open to change will take you out of your comfort zone and into the realm of exponential success.

## Assessing the Value of Change

The fundamental principle of change is making a difference. If you desire to see changes in your life, you (and only you) will be the catalyst to do so. It really comes down to first changing how you think. Our reality is based on our dominant thoughts and what we accept as our truth. For each individual, that truth is unique. Your dominant thoughts will change throughout your life — but you can direct these changes to go in the direction you choose. You will learn this skill later in the book as you master the art of change.

Throughout life, change is your only constant. Your body will change, your beliefs will change, your lifestyle will change, and inevitably your goals will change. View change positively. With practice, you can master creating and accepting change without fear. It is common for fear and change to be partners in crime because people fear the unknown. If you work to see the change you seek, you will find that change is not only acceptable, but also desired.

Change is inevitable; it's necessary and normal. As we grow and mature, projecting change into the universe gives the universe the chance to bring new opportunities back to us. It is like a game of tennis, with you serving first. Put it out there, serve it to the universe, and get excited for the changes being sent your way.

Careful thought and planning is required. Begin by spending time with your journal or just some pen and paper. This process of discovery will help you to not only evaluate change, but to understand exactly how you want this change to appear in your life.

My business, and my life, were changing rapidly and required a plan. Writing was a great way for me to understand where I needed change in order to get what I wanted. Thoughts create ideas and ideas create the action plan necessary for the change to occur.

A great example of this process is when someone decides to get healthy. Once the idea takes shape, change – whether physical or dietary in nature – is necessary to reach the end goal. Through commitment and repetition, that plan of action reshapes their body into their desired vision.

When you initiate a positive change in your life, you are telling the universe to send more positive experiences in your direction. In fact, making positive changes in your life eliminates lingering fears as you gain confidence and begin to have a more positive outlook. Gaining positive momentum transforms things that used to seem difficult or insurmountable into possibilities, but it takes strength to always look for the positive in life and overcome these obstacles.

## Change: Making It Happen

By now, I am hopeful that you are nodding your head in agreement, excited about your own potential for change. Now it is time to become the difference–maker in your own life and serve up that first change to the universe.

> "If you don't like something, change it. If you can't change it, change your attitude."
>
> Maya Angelou

The process for making a positive change in your life can be summed up in three easy steps:

**Step 1:** Deciding that you need to change, and what to change.

**Step 2:** Choosing when to change, and how you would like to change.

**Step 3:** Having the vision of what the change will provide.

The changes you make will be specific to your own life. Don't procrastinate. Change requires momentum and benefits from constant and immediate attention. There is great value in seeing how other people enact change, so I am sharing my journey to help you understand your own path more clearly.

My business required change to adjust its direction and support new opportunities. The need for change was created by the vision I adopted from one of my mentors. He pushed me to consider any and all opportunities in my path, and that influenced me. Not knowing what I didn't know led me to assess the opportunity in plain view through research and the discovery process.

*This is crucial to your success.*

Ask lots of questions and review the process several times to ensure you understand what is required to make the best decision possible. I immediately started evaluating the cost opportunity, which consisted of looking at the revenue potential of these new business processes. Sales is essential for all companies, so with my expertise this shift was easy for me. Seeing the potential in this new endeavor, I made an immediate decision that change was needed. When my business was properly positioned for that change, a strategy was formed outlining what the change would provide.

This process has been followed for everything in my life. Evaluate and pay attention to how you feel in situations and then discern information to organize the facts into relevant categories. I achieved a great deal using this process. You will learn more about the steps to make great decisions later in this book.

## Learning from the Game Changers

We all have come into contact with people, or game changers, who truly make a difference. People who have not only changed their own paths, but have often changed the lives and journeys of others. True game changers are not content to continue traveling down the same, familiar path, they forge ahead, breaking new ground as they go.

I have encountered many game changers throughout my life. One who really stood out was my friend Paul who, at age 22, was just starting a business creating supplements in the health and wellness industry.

He was a shy guy working at a bodybuilding store while building his business in his free time. He invited me over to watch a game one night and I was blown away by the fact that I was hanging with a twenty–three–year–old millionaire. We talked about his struggle to start his business and he admitted that the legal challenges he faced actually led to his innovative distribution plan. To gain a broader customer base, free of the governmental regulations in his native Canada, Paul created a mail–order startup company. Though the beginning was onerous, he persevered, creating the largest bodybuilding supplement manufacturer in the world – its most well known product being HydroxyCut.

> "If you do not change direction, you may end up where you are heading."
>
> Lao Tzu

Paul possessed all the qualities of success, and that is what eventually made him so successful. The manner in which he spoke, the way his mind processed information, and his resiliency and relentless desire to reach his goals proved to me that when you believe in your vision, your belief will fuel your drive.

He's not the only game changer I am lucky enough to know. Tony seized a great opportunity, seeing too little competition among Canadian cellular phone providers. He took on the established phone companies and started a new cellular service with new, innovative pricing models that the market desperately needed. It shook up the industry! In only six years, Wind Mobile continues to disrupt the industry, increasing its market share by appealing to consumers' needs for great service with fair, straightforward pricing.

Change fueled the opportunity for Tony's success, and he quickly identified that the cell phone industry needed a great change. He realized he could operate profitably by offering lower prices than his established and high priced competition. There were finally more valuable solutions to choose from, and his customer base exploded. Tony took on big business, and created a lot of controversy in doing so, but he changed the game.

Vishen is another game changer who has been highly influential. He started a technology–based company called Mind Valley that introduces wellness, mindfulness and personal development into educational platforms.

Vishen launched Mind Valley in 2003 as a digital publisher and marketer of self–help programs from his New York apartment. In 2005, he decided to return to his native Malaysia, relocating his business to Kuala Lumpur and adding 40 employees to his team. By 2012, Vishen had over 150 employees and continues to contribute to the Malaysian economy while maintaining his company's global presence. Today Mind Valley has been a featured company on GameChangers 500, attracting authors and entrepreneurs from all over the world.

Vishen and Mind Valley have changed the industry and created the opportunity for many less–known authors and speakers to successfully launch their services and products globally. This is a game changer not only for Vishen, but for all of his collaborators who come to him with a dream.

Most game changers share a common trait: they boldly move forward in their respective fields of interests when they see an opportunity. They see the end goal and keep it in mind always. The examples are vast and endless, spanning a large spectrum of industries and businesses. Here are a few other great examples of game changers to check out:

- Robert Kalin – www.etsy.com
- Siobhan Neilland – www.onemama.org
- Shari Arison – www.miya–water.com
- Lauren Walters & Will Hauser – www.twodegreesfood.com
- Charles Adler, Perry Chen & Yancey Strickler – www.kickstarter.com

Think about the people we met in this chapter. What made them special? What made them unique? From my perspective, it is their endless desire to follow what Gandhi suggested: "You must be the change you wish to see in the world."

That attitude fuels the pure and passionate yearning for great levels of success. The same is true for you. You can be a game changer and leave a significant footprint on the world. But you must first dedicate yourself to identifying the change you want to see and then serving it up to the universe.

**Playbook Exercise 3:**

Journal your answers to the following questions:

1.  With the game changers we discussed in this chapter, what made them unique?

2.  What traits do you believe you share with these game changers?

3.  What traits of theirs would you like to see more of in yourself?

4.  How would you like to "change the game?"

**Success Meditation # 3: – Preparing For Change**

www.ChristopherCumby.com/SuccessMeditation

**JOURNAL NOTES:**

_____

_____

_____

_____

_____

_____

_____

_____

_____

_____

_____

_____

_____

_____

_____

_____

_____

_____

**JOURNAL NOTES:**

_____

_____

_____

_____

_____

_____

_____

_____

_____

_____

_____

_____

_____

_____

_____

_____

# 4 The Fourth Pillar: Know Why You Want Something (*Make the Why Big Enough*)

> *"There are two great days in a person's life –*
> *the day we are born and the day we find out why."*
>
> William Barclay

We often ask the simple question: "*Why?*" While a seemingly small word, the power of uttering it is immense. Many would agree that it is the easiest question to ask and the hardest to answer. Scholars have dedicated their lives to answering this question, spending their entire careers looking for some semblance of an explanation.

As human beings, we have collectively worked to analyze, evaluate, and identify our internal and external *why*. Yet we still remain in the dark, unable to offer an exact answer to this difficult question.

Consider the time and energy devoted to questions such as:

- *Why are we here?*
- *Why is this happening?*
- *Why now?*
- *Why me?*

These are deep, and sometimes philosophical, questions. We may never fully understand these complex *whys*, but we continue to search for answers, not settling until we find some sense of clarity.

## Defining the *Why*

The answer to any *why* begins in our imagination with a sense of wonder. Just as children spend their early years discovering and creating, we must have that same sense of wonder to find the answers to our own *why*.

This concept of creating a big *why* may represent the most important chapter in the book for you to understand and apply. Learning the fundamentals of achievement, coaches and mentors will encourage you to focus your attention on your *why*. There is incredible value in understanding why you want something, be it an object or feeling, and how it will motivate your behavior. It will be driven through thought and

> "The true sign of intelligence is not knowledge, but imagination."
> Albert Einstein

transformed into a feeling, or a frequency. Implementing a big *why* will support your goals, your dreams and your aspirations.

Thoughts become energy, and energy is made up of frequencies in their most basic form. These vibrating frequencies join together and form tangible and meaningful results within our lives. The law of attraction suggests that all "like" frequencies are drawn to one another, demonstrating why it is crucial to positively focus your thoughts.

> "Whatever we plant in our subconscious mind and then nourish with repetition and emotion will one day become a reality."
> Earl Nightingale

Everything in our known world has a frequency, as both Thomas Edison and Albert Einstein professed. We now know that our human brain emits a frequency and is both a transmitter and receiver of such energy. Using the full capacity of focused thought, carried out with power and intensity, is how we manifest what we want in life. This supports and enables our why. It gives our why the momentum to look for more in our lives.

We all want to be happy – that happiness is generated through our emotional frequency. When we imagine ourselves being happy, it creates the possibility in our minds. With constant focus and belief, along with the necessary action, we create and attract these possibilities into our reality, or design another possibility to pursue as we uncover more facts along the way. Facts are the cornerstones that support your *why*, and a huge part of the foundation of success.

*Why* is closely tied to the other pillars, each one ensures the *why* remains clear. When reasons are unclear, you'll find that your foundation weakens, appears unstable and will no longer support your *why*. It has been said that as many as 98 percent of people drift through their lives never experiencing the life they really want to live. Is that an accurate statistic? Think about your circle of friends. Doesn't everyone have at least one "Oh, I wish I would have …" story? Be the one who goes after what you want. Move to the new city, take that job, visit that country – whatever it is you're dreaming of, go after it!

Dreams, goals and aspirations (DGAs) uplift you and bring happiness, creating the big *whys* in life. Imagine living your *why* and encouraging it with a positive mindset. You'll be in a position to confidently take action and you'll notice that the right people, events and opportunities start appearing. The "have" and "have not" mentalities both require energy, choose which path to focus yours on and begin creating the life you want today.

## The Segments of *Why*

Why are all success stories based on someone having a goal, dream or aspiration? These DGAs are all formed by our imagination. As your ideas become reality, you'll soon discover that behind all accomplishments lies a purpose. Keeping your thoughts and attitudes positive will allow opportunities to align with your purpose as you start achieving your DGAs.

Your *whys* in life are closely tied to what makes you happy. In fact, I have found that achieving DGAs makes people the happiest. Remember this as you search for your *why*.

My dream of becoming an author and mentor was rooted in my desire to help others; it is my chief aim in life. I armed myself with the facts, took action and visualized my next logical steps. My life, as I imagined it, began to unfold before me.

When beginning your search for your DGAs, ask yourself:

1. What is the purpose?
2. Is this aligned with my chief aim?
3. Do I believe in its outcome?

This exercise focuses the mind. It identifies the goal, assesses its feasibility and lets us remove doubts of whether or not our DGAs can be achieved. Our frequency, or energy level, can be elevated to match what we are seeking.

Love what you do. A positive vibration will continually attract new opportunities for growth at exactly the right time. Create a big enough *why* and nothing will keep you down. When your purpose (your *why*) is aligned with your positive momentum, you'll see change. Positive change. Meaningful change. Life–altering change.

Let's pause here for a moment to better understand the power you already possess. The method we just discussed creates new neuro–pathways, or thought patterns. When the ones you have don't serve you, form new ones.

How do you know you are focused on what you want? Well, how do you feel when you think about it? Most people believe they are thinking about what they want, but they aren't paying enough attention to exactly how they feel. Since feeling is matched with thought, creating a specific frequency, they are likely sending out a frequency of "lack" – of not having what they want.

**TIP** – When you think about what you want, feel good while you're thinking about it. Find a calm place and think positively about your reaching your DGAs. If not, you will subconsciously create a block. Set your objectives and know what you want; it will appear in your life. It's a simple concept, yes, but it takes practice to change your mindset – directing what happens in your life instead of simply reacting to them.

As I began building my business, doubts and fears came charging in. I thought about what would happen if my ideas or plans didn't work. My mentor pushed me to refocus my attention, concentrating instead on what I really wanted, allowing more opportunities to come my way. As a result, I focused on being a great salesperson, which led me to sell more, which attracted more clients.

## Your *Why* Is Not Your *How*

Most people are not trained in the art of journaling. Without taking the proper time to reflect and plan ahead, people's DGAs are often met with defeat before taking the first step. This is undoubtedly due to their mind skipping to how before fully believing in their why.

**How** – The skills, process, action steps, techniques, plans, and activities taken for manifestation of your DGAs. This is not, however, where you should focus your dominant thoughts and attention. Paying attention to the *how* is why most people give up on their dreams. Fear and doubt take over and without the four pillars, the dream is over before it ever begins.

I discovered this rule early in my career. I knew I wanted to use my sales skills, but I didn't know how to reach the lucrative goal I had set for myself. I dove into an industry with which I had no prior experience to create exactly what I wanted, knowing *why* I wanted it.

The company I worked for had numerous incentives, and many of them came in the form of travel, requiring employees to sell enough business to achieve all–expense–paid trips to exotic, international destinations. I was in heaven since I loved sales and I loved to travel. Because of this, my *why* was aligned. I sold more business than any other salesperson for the years I was with them. It was easy to reach this goal since my *why* was enormously strong.

One thing is certain: if I had focused on *how* I was going to live the lifestyle I wanted, it would have consumed me. I would have spent too much energy focusing on my lack and how to overcome it and I wouldn't have had any energy left to actually do my job. Too often we get hung up on how something will occur, putting us in a position to make excuses. We say things like "How will I ever get there?" By focusing on *how*, we allow *how* to be a cloud, covering up our *why*. It is your *why* that motivates you to fulfill your goals.

**TIP – Don't confuse your *how* with your *why*.** Your *why* is what keeps you going. Your *how* matters, but don't let it be a crutch. *How* lets you make excuses and can limit you. Cast aside your doubts and decide to reach your goals and you'll find that success is at your fingertips.

Don't get hung up on the *how*, be confident in your ability to achieve.

### Attitude is Everything

Having a positive attitude is like having a straight flush in a poker game; it pretty much guarantees you a win over the competition. I have found that when your attitude is on point, the facts are easier to discern and you become more aware of what makes you happy. Within each of us lies an inherent ability to overcome facts and position our lives to attract fantastic success – but only if our attitude reflects our goals.

> "Develop an attitude of gratitude, and give thanks for everything that happens to you, knowing that every step forward is a step toward achieving something bigger and better than your current situation."
>
> Brian Tracy

Here is a great example: I attended a party several years ago. The minute I walked into the room I felt drawn to several people I had never met. I approached them and started talking. I connected with new people, made professional contacts and created new opportunities for my business.

This party is still one of the best and most memorable events I have ever attended.

Why?

My company had just closed a million–dollar commission earlier that day, and my attitude at the party was elevated. I attracted more frequencies and opportunities vibrating on the same level as me. Coincidentally, I saw a few other people I knew from that same party a few days later. Their experience was not nearly as enjoyable. I discovered they had recently been hit with an unexpected expense and as a result, their energy levels, outlooks and vibrations were all very low because they had been focused on their problem. They attracted an experience that matched their feelings and frequencies. It influenced their interactions and how they engaged with others.

I noticed that when my attitude was positively elevated, I experienced a better outlook on life – resonating above the noise of negativity and attracting friends with higher vibrations and similar moods. Take a good look at who you spend time with and how you feel when you are around them. **This is key to your success**. Creating a harmonious environment conducive to your DGAs should be your first objective.

Maintaining a positive attitude enables you to discern facts from opinions more efficiently and accurately. Seek facts from positive people who possess a higher frequency than others. They will assist you faster than listening to just any mere opinion. Your *why* should be reinforced with facts, as you learned earlier. When you are able to collect, absorb, recall, and judge the facts, you will think more strategically and better solutions will appear in your life. Aligning your attitude with your positive thought process is like having a personal guide through life. Whatever makes you happy should be developed and pursued.

Let's consider Mother Teresa, an individual who used this process to bring love, selflessness, and charity to the world around her. She brought attention to the plight of impoverished people and made a positive, global impact on their behalf. She had a high vibration and frequency because she fulfilled her own inner desire to help others. Her level of success was in exact proportion, if not greater, than her level of commitment and belief in what she did.

Wouldn't you agree that Mother Teresa lived a life with a big enough *why*? She lived simply, possessed no worldly goods and had no wealth, yet she lived a life of abundance. The money she required to feed and nurture others came to her when it was needed, and she was able to live a beautiful life in servitude to God and those in need.

Mother Teresa's *why* appeared at a very early age, and she pursued it despite the difficulties she faced. She devoted her life to serving God, to serving the sick and hungry and to encouraging the world to do unto others as you would have them do unto you. Her passionate dedication to helping others continues to inspire people the world over.

How about larger–than–life personal development coach Brendon Burchard? His story captured the attention of his readers. Brendon nearly died in a car accident at the age of 19 while traveling with a friend in the Dominican Republic. It was after this traumatic experience that he decided to pursue a life worth living, creating a *why* that would inspire millions.

With great effort, persistence, and a thirst for knowledge, Brendon has become one of the most widely followed and most successful personal development experts in the world.

Another amazing individual who found his why was the great Zig Ziglar. This man has inspired millions with some of the most brilliant messaging about living with integrity ever created. Zig was one of the biggest names in motivational speaking, sharing this passion and excitement for helping others for over forty years.

Zig stumbled into his vocation after being encouraged by his former boss and mentor. He wrote his first book in 1975, called *See You at the Top*, and went on to author more than thirty books during his lifetime. He had a gift for motivating others, having first learned how to motivate himself.

His stories have resonated with people all over the world, from all walks of life, and that is why Zig loved what he did. He discovered his why, journeying into the world of inspirational and motivational speaking with immense joy.

If you haven't heard one of Zig's talks, I encourage you to find one online and listen. Zig was a forefather of personal achievement. He said, "*If you dream it, you can achieve it.*" We are all dreamers. And if we dream big about our *why*, we can create outstanding results in our lives.

One of my favorite stories is about Scott Neeson, a former president of 20th Century Fox who gave it all up to found the Cambodian Children's Fund. Visiting Cambodia and seeing the horrific living conditions of hundreds of families inspired Scott to make a drastic change. He quit his high paying, high profile job, sold everything he had and moved to Cambodia to dedicate his life to helping these children and their families move beyond the toxic dumps of steel and plastic in their country.

Scott knew he had discovered his purpose, and with great vision and tireless effort, he changed the lives of these children and their families. These children now have access to education, clean water, and fresh food and are learning new ways to cultivate and clean their once decaying environment. With a very big *why*, Scott found something he could really feel good about, something that was going to make a lasting impact for those who needed help.

These stories highlight people who were jolted into their *big why* in life. They all had big reasons why they pursued their own ambitions but each of them has one thing in common: they help others.

This is why it is crucial to learn, understand, and apply the pillars to your every day life. Practice the pillars daily, as we will build upon them as we progress through your success playbook. As we continue, we will expand your physical, emotional, intellectual, and spiritual self and discover ideas and individuals to support and encourage you on your life's journey.

> "Everyone has been made for a particular work;
> and the desire for that work has been put in every heart."
>
> Rumi

It is your *why* that keeps you moving forward. It keeps you motivated, dedicated, and determined to reach so far that you simply cannot fail. Success remains within your reach, and evaluating how things will happen will never keep you from making things happen.

### Playbook Exercise 4:

1. Having read the four pillars of success, write out each pillar in your own words. Commit to using them daily. Make it a habit, and with repetition, they will connect you to your DGAs.

2. Identify your *big why*. What are your DGAs?

   a. Need help finding your big why? Attend an event. Do some research and ask others what areas they are passionate about. Find a coach or mentor. Read new books. Get out of your comfort zone and try new things. Live life with an open mind to the possibilities that surround you.

3. Is anything holding you back from taking the first step towards your DGAs? If so, what is it? What steps can you take to overcome it?

4. Finally, listen to the meditation in the link below to calm your mind and open your thoughts.

### Success Meditation #4 – Universal Mind

www.ChristopherCumby.com/SuccessMeditation

**JOURNAL NOTES:**

_____

_____

_____

_____

_____

_____

_____

_____

_____

_____

_____

_____

_____

_____

_____

_____

_____

_____

**JOURNAL NOTES:**

_____

_____

_____

_____

_____

_____

_____

_____

_____

_____

_____

_____

_____

_____

_____

_____

_____

_____

# 5 Becoming the Creator: How to Take Responsibility for this Role

Movement is an essential part of your journey. Until now, we have discussed crucial aspects of your life that prevent movement. That is, our attention has been focused on building a foundation stabilized by four rock–solid pillars. This foundation and these pillars prevent the house you build from swaying, cracking, and, ultimately, crumbling down around you.

But now we shift. The goal of this shift is to empower you to create your own life. As a creator, you have an enormous responsibility with fantastic potential. You can manifest whatever you choose. There are no limitations, and you certainly do not have to ask for permission. As long as you can see it, visualize it, or even dream it, it can be yours. Let's begin the process of creating.

Do not confuse construction with creation. We *construct* a foundation and pillars to support what we *create*. We have the ability to love what we create long before we actually create it. The more we love something, the greater our likelihood of creating it.

No one can create for you as well as *you*. With a balanced heart, body, and soul you hold the key to your dreams. Once you accept that, life as you know it will drastically change. You will discover that nothing happens to you unless you create it – making you the creator of the things in your life, whether good or bad. The outcome is what you choose.

> "The whole difference between construction and creation is exactly this: that a thing constructed can only be loved after it is constructed; but a thing created is loved before it exists."
>
> Charles Dickens

Learning the concept of "nothing happens to me unless I create it," opened my eyes to the fact that we each possess much greater potential than merely struggling through life. Everything that happens does so because of a choice we make. Using our imagination, we can create our life and design our own path by asking better questions.

Imagine for a moment the ability to create whatever it is you dream up in your mind. Now, assuming you always follow the Golden Rule and reflect positivity, you will attain your DGAs. You are composed of energies, frequencies and vibrations that connect you to everything and everyone. Choosing a path that damages someone else, whether physically or mentally, also means damaging yourself. So the Golden Rule pushes each of us to coexist and support one another.

## The Five C's

The 5 C's of your character can be controlled and once they are, you will learn to command what you want and have faith that you will receive it.

### 1. Confidence

The first necessary component of your character (or the person you project into the world) is **confidence**. Most people fear criticism; it is actually a major fear that keeps people from acting on ideas they imagine. They dismantle they lack. They don't believe in their idea because they lack the confidence to take one step and seek out the facts to support it. Often the facts are right in front of their eyes. People immediately go into their own recall system to find information (their own beliefs) to support their thinking. Coming up empty, they demolish the idea and it never takes root.

Confidence is like a muscle, it requires exercise to grow strong. To personally conquer the fear of criticism, I ask others what bothers them about me. It's uncomfortable, very uncomfortable, but really productive. I figure that by asking people and then identifying something I can improve upon, I can break negative vibrations or patterns. Choose people who will give you honest and straightforward chance and leave your comfort zone. Outside your comfort zone, in that awkward, unfamiliar space, the magic happens and you can live each day to the fullest.

*How do you know if you never try?*

## 2.  Commitment

Another component of higher character is your willingness to **commit** and take action. A lack of action is what keeps people from achieving their DGAs. They try once or twice, find it too hard or are met with a challenge, and then lose the motivation to continue. Dream big. Commit to your goal. Take action. If you live by the words "*if it is meant to be, it is up to me*," you will see the greatness within you emerge.

## 3.  Creativity

**Creativity** is a crucial part of success. Writing in your journal is such a simple, powerful way to unlock your creative thinking. Creation begins with a vision, or goal, that you launch into the atmosphere through thought. Writing allows you to unleash your imagination and create opportunities from your ideas that resonate with you and make you feel good.

Creativity should feel natural. I look at my own children for ideas, as they possess such power in their imagination, often reminding me of how I once did as well. This helps me stay imaginative.

Being creative is more than just having new ideas; it is also reimagining your own growth and potential. You are a *creative being*; you truly are what you think about. Your life is represented by your dominant thoughts.

Engaging your creativity expands the realm of possibilities and is crucial to your success.

## 4. Clarity

So many people suffer from a lack of **clarity**. They drift through life with an incredible amount of indecision. If you find yourself wandering aimlessly, are you lacking clarity about where you want to go? People who succeed share an essential trait: they know where they want to go.

## 5. Credibility

> "Real integrity is doing the right thing, knowing that nobody's going to know whether you did it or not."
>
> Oprah Winfrey

Credible creators are the most successful kind. As a creator, you control your own **credibility**. You and you alone are responsible for being true to your word. Do what you say you're going to do. Work towards your DGAs. So as you plan your own creation, do it in a way that's reflective of the character you want to project to the world. Achieving your dreams takes work, but being a credible creator will allow you to attract more positivity, collaboration, support and success.

## Becoming Attracted to the Law of Attraction

Modern science suggests that our energetic field is connected to everything. We are more than just skin and bones with a brain. We are beings with extraordinary skills.

In her book *The Field: The Quest for the Secret Force of the Universe*, author Lynne McTaggart investigates this secret force and interviewed leading scientists around the globe to share facts and prove this new discovery.

McTaggart's interviews reveal a radical new paradigm – that the human mind and body are not separate from the environment surrounding them, but instead merge their energy with the collective frequencies and vibrations all around us. This discovery suggests that human consciousness is interconnected.

What is the law of attraction? The law of attraction is basically *like attracts like*: focusing on positive or negative thoughts will bring about positive or negative results. The simplest way to understand the complexity of this law is to think of it like this: how you feel, good or bad, sends out a vibration and frequency that is looking for similar vibrations and frequencies. That is why it pays to be positive even when you think you have no reason to be. The law works with either negative energy or positive energy; it is completely unbiased. It will bring other frequencies to the strongest frequency you are broadcasting. You are the creator of your life, but you are certainly not alone in your journey. Creation welcomes guests, and those guests can help you set the table for success or completely ruin the party. The law of attraction helps you invite the right guests.

This is a good time to take a look at your life. Is there anything that feels bad that's being reflected in your life? If so, your dominant thoughts are creating it. If things are going really well for you, is there something you would like to explore further? Challenge yourself. Be creative. This chapter's playbook exercise will help you evaluate what you attract and help you improve upon what you have achieved.

The most successful creators take full responsibility for what they create, no matter the circumstances. By using the laws that govern creation, you will understand why your emotional frequency created your reality. Being the creator offers the opportunity to change what you don't like and elevate what makes you happy. Welcome more of what deeply resonates with you and deflect anything that impedes that connection.

We all have what it takes to be a creator. We don't lack any of the qualities we need to become true difference–makers. We simply need guidance to become more accurate in building a life that makes us happy.

## A Leap of Faith and a Major Shift

When I turned 30, my life took a major shift – I was divorced, had literally nothing left to my name and still had to provide for my child. I felt like a big fat failure.

But was I, really?

I realized that leaving a bad situation, although uncomfortable, would lead me away from what I knew was a dead end street. I knew in my heart that my current situation was not supporting my DGAs. I knew I wasn't the person I wanted to be. So I took the leap of faith and left. I could create something better. What a great decision that turned out to be, despite its many challenges. I believed that I was here to live out my purpose and that this experience would render something good for my future. It did. I became a better person, a better husband, a better dad, and today I have a beautiful wife, four awesome kids, and a life that I designed.

Growing up, I always asked myself: *Who will I become?* I thought of it often, and in fact, I still do. I learned who I am by tracking my thoughts, writing my goals down and creating my vision of the future. I have made it my mission to help others discover their personal success stories.

Secrets to success are in plain sight and the law of attraction is one of these secrets. It is everywhere and costs nothing to use, yet it provides each of us with tremendous opportunities to live a life that truly makes us happy. You are using the law of attraction in your life already and your experiences, good or bad, are the direct result of the frequency you broadcast. You attract similar vibrations in return. When you unlock your awareness of this law and use it for a positive attraction, backing it up with a positive mindset, your reality will start to reflect your chief aim in life (purpose) and inspire your dominant thoughts and focus. You will become what you want to become.

> "What lies behind you and what lies in front of you pales in comparison to what lies inside you."
>
> Ralph Waldo Emerson

**Ask yourself:** *Are my energy and beliefs mostly negative or positive?* If the answer is positive, well done. Remain focused and persistent. If negative, let's shift your attention to using the law of attraction to your advantage.

The law requires a frequency, and you represent this frequency when you think thoughts that make you feel good, or bad. Ever notice how someone with a negative outlook on life/work/relationships tends to stay in that rut? Have you ever had to disassociate from someone because their attitude and energy was just too negative? That's a negative frequency and the good news is – it can be reversed.

Studying, understanding and applying the law of attraction will bring abundance. It's a game changer and the possibilities are endless. As a creator, what type of frequency are you sending? Do you need to change it?

**Aligning Your Frequency**

In college, I was introduced to the concept of thoughts being made of energy. Aligning yourself with your chief aim/purpose should feel natural. Your life should be in harmony with your environment. These conditions it will attract the right circumstances, events, people and opportunities.

But what if it is not in harmony? What if you are not aligned, or feel as though you're wandering aimlessly? If so, consider neuro–linguistic programming (NLP). I discovered this practice more than 20 years ago and have had the privilege of working with an esteemed NLP coach for the last decade.

61

So what exactly is NLP? It's an approach to communication, personal development and psychotherapy that lets you dive deeper into your subconscious and plant the seeds necessary for positive attraction. Personally, it helped me rid myself of deep–rooted negative beliefs that I had carried through life. An NLP coach can be instrumental in guiding you through the layers of your life, unlocking keys to true passions and your genius zone. Delving deep into your subconscious mind will help you discover what you really love and what excites you. NLP helped me understand what was holding me back, such as my own criticism, which helped me to crush these self–made blocks.

The basis of any of these behaviors and decisions is being fully responsible and recognizing that you have complete and utter control of your life. This is when you will discover the creator inside and be introduced to your *other self*. Your other self is the version of you, and your life, that you desire and envision. Being true to what you believe in, you'll inevitably meet with some opposition. Remember that you create every experience and can also undo it. But it takes practice. Practice enough and your behaviors will become habits.

Once you identify what bothers you, ask questions about how it can be changed. The answers will appear, and you will be able to hone in on the real blocks once you know they exist. It's funny how problems seem to disappear when you give them no power.

We all want to live a meaningful and successful life. We may define success differently, but it is a goal we all choose to meet.

As a creator, wake up each day and make the decision to move your feet forward and manifest a life filled with high purpose, extensive character, and enormous potential.

We are all creators. Simple as that.

**Playbook Exercise 5:**

Grab your journal and let's explore the following questions:

1. Are your energy and beliefs mostly negative or positive?

2. Write some of them down. Take a moment to reflect on them. How can you improve upon them?

3. Are you operating at a frequency that resonates at a high level?

4. What steps can you take to elevate your frequency?

5. Is there anything that feels bad that's being reflected in your life?

6. If things are going really well for you, is there something you would like to explore further?

7. How can you start applying the 5 C's to your life?

   - Confidence
   - Commitment
   - Creativity
   - Clarity
   - Credibility

8. What type of creator will you be?

Good questions are critical to provoking our creative giant that lies within. Our mind is inquisitive and loves to resolve questions; journaling your thoughts will help you find your genius zone.

## Success Meditation #5: – Infinite Mind Connection

www.ChristopherCumby.com/SuccessMeditation

**JOURNAL NOTES:**

_____

_____

_____

_____

_____

_____

_____

_____

_____

_____

_____

_____

_____

_____

_____

_____

_____

_____

**JOURNAL NOTES:**

_____

_____

_____

_____

_____

_____

_____

_____

_____

_____

_____

_____

_____

_____

_____

_____

_____

_____

_____

# 6  Know Yourself:
## The Who A.R.E. You? Principle

> *In order for your life to change,*
> *you must first be the change.*

This statement resonates. It is simple, but may possibly be the most powerful realization that you uncover in your life.

Many people live their lives waiting for the universe to bring them good luck. These people do not see that they have the power to change their lives. Take action and ownership for your destiny and create your own luck. Dig deeply within yourself to find answers. It won't be easy, it will take a lot of practice and repetition, but it will change the direction of your life.

When I began seeking change in my life, it was at a time of despair (which is common for many people). I was down on my luck, I had lost most of my savings, and for a long time, I blamed other people and circumstances for my situation. Then, at this critical moment, I had an epiphany. I realized that I had the power to change the direction of my life. So I stopped feeling sorry for myself and took action.

With this realization I created the *Who A.R.E. You?* principle. This simple acronym will reprogram your thought process to increase your awareness. Knowing who you are is crucial to living a fulfilling and meaningful life; so let's take a look at ourselves and find out.

What exactly is *Who A.R.E. You?*

### A is for **Attitude**

- There is a reason that most personal development professionals reference this – success requires a positive attitude. It is the energy that attracts the right motivation into our lives for tackling our goals. Seeing the positive side of any situation will separate you from the masses and provide you with strength when you need it the most. Staying positive puts you in control of situations where you would otherwise be powerless. Living a life full of positivity, you will easily overcome adversity and appreciate roadblocks for what they are – steppingstones to success!

### R is for **Responsibility**

- As we discussed in chapter five, taking responsibility for what happens to you gives you control over your outcomes. Take ownership for your life and hold yourself accountable. Responsibility is achieved when you realize you create your reality and control your destiny. It may be uncomfortable initially, but once you stop placing blame on external circumstances and look within yourself for answers, the progress you make toward reaching your goal will astound you.

### E is for **Emotion**

- Our emotions are directly linked to our subconscious frequency; this powerful energy is how we manifest our reality. The strength of your emotional control is a direct representation of what you can successfully accomplish. Control your emotions and you'll find yourself in alignment with your higher purpose. Developing this emotional intelligence will give you with a clearer view of the world around you, showing you the steps needed to live a life of abundance.

The *Who A.R.E. You?* principle coincides with your daily activity and provides a framework for you to follow. Getting in the habit of checking in with your *attitude*, *responsibility*, and *emotion*, will keep you in tune with your inner thoughts.

Here is an example of how this principle works. A question I am frequently asked is "How are you?" In fact, this may be the most commonly asked question in the world. When asked this question, I apply the *A.R.E.* acronym and remind myself to have a positive *attitude* and not share in any negativity, be aware of my *responsibility*, and remember my *emotional* frequency is being sent out into the world.

**BOOM!** You can apply this principle to virtually any interaction or decision you have to make throughout the day. It becomes habit and will place you in complete control of your responses and reactions. The *Who A.R.E. You?* principle is incredibly effective and I have taught this philosophy for the past decade.

Implementing this principle into your daily thought process, you will discover the ability to self–assess every day. When you learn *Who You A.R.E.*, you will learn more about what you want. You will raise your vibration, and you'll be able to make decisions quickly and take responsibility for every outcome. You will tap into your internal emotional guidance system, which will in turn guide you to your dreams and define your purpose as you grow.

The *Who A.R.E. You?* principle will transform your life. When you have a positive attitude your level of responsibility is elevated, supporting the emotional frequency you'll experience. Start slowly. Implement the principle with small decisions and then progress to using it for larger decisions and defining your core values and goals. The *Who A.R.E. You?* principle creates the necessary habits of a positive *attitude*, which will help you to understand how to take *responsibility* for your life, which will help you to recognize the ability to command your *emotions*. Through perfecting these skills, you can learn to remain on constant alert for opportunities that align with your DGAs.

### Owning Your Life

*Without knowing who you are, how can you truly know where you are going?* This question should be important to anyone looking to identify their purpose. Not knowing who we are or where we are going can lead to unhappiness and depression. Thankfully, there is a solution.

Let's take weight control and health as an example and assume you feel bad that you're out of shape. Start by listing the things you would like to do to make yourself feel better – walking, working out, yoga, running, eating healthy, etc. When you write it, *you now own it*. Now you can take action and manifest this new reality. By doing this, the new positive habit you are focused on takes the place of the old habit.

Once you start searching for what empowers you, you will be alerted to opportunities that support your vision. Your mind will be focused on things that support the same frequency as your DGAs and you'll notice that people who support your goals will start to appear.

Identify your pain points. What emotions do you exhibit when faced with stress or adversity? What emotions would you rather exhibit? These answers will guide you through your own *Who A.R.E. You?* process.

With *Who A.R.E. You?*, stick to the basics, keep things simple and you will experience fewer distractions. It will allow you to evolve naturally into the DGAs that you want in your life.

### Knowledge Through Discovery

Understanding *Who You A.R.E.* is part of the discovery and wonder that forge the pathway to knowledge. You have the ability to dismantle doubt and fear by becoming definitive in your thoughts and actions. With the principles in this chapter, you now know that controlling your emotions to support your decisions will point you in the direction of your dreams.

With this established, let's look at how the *A.R.E.* principle imparts knowledge and wisdom. Imagine for a moment that someone is berating you in public. Turn your attention to the first part of the acronym, *attitude*. In most cases, people would immediately think of this situation as negative, but what if you turned that around?

Think positively for a moment while staying connected to the belittlement you're feeling. If you remained positive, what do you think would happen to the negative energy being directed at you? It would dissipate because your energy didn't fuel its fire. It would become irrelevant and unimportant because you were able to maintain a positive attitude. This is a major turning point, as you are now in control of the outcome of a situation in which you may have previously felt powerless. You maintained a positive *attitude*, took *responsibility* for your reaction, and used your *emotions* to better the situation.

**Ask yourself:** When you look at your goals, what do you feel? This feeling is the quickest way to determine if your goal is aligned with your current beliefs. Let's assume you feel good for a moment. The goal you have set means you don't have it yet, so this is the moment you focus your attention on your *attitude*. Stay positive and believe you can achieve it, no matter what happens.

Now determine the things you can control in the following days, weeks, months, and years – that is, your focus or *responsibility*. Is your attention devoted to the realization of your DGAs? Keep your dominant thoughts on the arrival of those DGAs. And make sure your *emotions* "feel good," if not, go back to the previous step's task or goal that you do feel good about. This will align you.

You will gain knowledge through your own experience, so be sure to apply this principle as much as possible to align *Who You A.R.E.* on a daily basis.

### *Who A.R.E. You?* – Step by Step

To fully integrate the *Who A.R.E. You?* principle into your life, here is an outline to maximize your strengths and improve your weaknesses in all four segments of the human being.

What *are* the four segments of the human being?

1. Physical
2. Intellectual
3. Emotional
4. Spiritual

The physical is your body, the vessel in which you inhabit the earth. The intellect is the invisible body, connected to thought and powered by the brain. It sends and receives information from the emotional body; invisible but connected to the physical through our internal organs, mainly the stomach and the vagus nerve (hence the phrase, "gut feeling"). The emotional body, through its support and relationship with the other bodies, forms our beliefs, and these beliefs are what get manifested into our reality.

When I developed the *Who A.R.E. You?* Principle, I had a "*Eureka!*" moment. I had finally met my other–self and realized that we're able to connect with the spiritual body through our subconscious mind.

So how do you connect with the subconscious mind? We actually do it every day. Our subconscious mind is like a filing cabinet with unlimited space. You can store incredible amounts of information, anything you pay attention to, really. Some files may only have one piece of data; these small files are easy to overlook and tend to get lost in the system. You have files that you access periodically; they have references so you can easily recall them. Then you have large, full files that consume most of the filing space and are used often. These files are so dominant they are what you think about most of the time.

But what about new ideas? Your new ideas start new files, and as you focus on gathering new pieces of information you can shift your focus to filling up these files. They can consume your thoughts and your thoughts create your reality. These files are your *habits*, the hypnotic rhythm of where you place your awareness. Paying attention to something and giving it energy results in creating new habits (files). You control the connection with your spiritual body and communication to the universe.

Living a life filled with unhealthy habits will create a negative connection to the universe. But if you live a life full of positive, healthy habits, you will manifest that type of connection with the universe. You have the power to choose.

### Give *Who You A.R.E.* Time to Emerge

When you identify with your DGAs and create a positive *attitude*, you take full *responsibility* for your life's outcome and connect with the higher frequency of *emotional* power necessary to be aware of your inner magic. Eventually all the corresponding ideas, people, places, events and tools will start to align for your greater good. Here is a word of caution: *give it time* and be patient; the universe works in mysterious and strange ways, and you must trust that things are unfolding exactly the way they need to.

> "Progress is impossible without change, and those who cannot change their minds cannot change anything."
>
> George Bernard Shaw

The *Who A.R.E. You?* Principle is a simple but effective thought process that, when fully applied, will revolutionize your life. You now have the tools to adopt this self–assessment method into your life, and through experience you will gain knowledge about your DGAs. This knowledge and wisdom will take you on a path of discovery that leads to living your best life!

## Playbook Exercise 6:

1. Let's write down how you *feel* – good or bad – for each of the following personal segments. Then list some actions/ideas you can implement to create new habits that support your DGAs. For each segment, think about actions that will make you feel better.

   - Physical
   - Intellectual
   - Emotional
   - Spiritual

   Is it taking up running with the intent to one day run a marathon? Maybe it's starting to practice yoga to calm your mind and find a spiritual connection? Intellectually, perhaps you'd like to start reading a book per month that will help you on your path to self–improvement?

2. Now let's apply the *Who A.R.E. You?* principle to connect with your desired outcome.

   - When you look at your goals, what do you feel? What is your *attitude*? Is it positive?

   - Now determine the things you can control in the following days, weeks, months, and years – that is your *responsibility*. Is your attention focused on the realization of your DGAs?

   - Do your *emotions* regarding your DGAs make you feel good? They should. If not, go back a step and reassess your responsibility list. If you still don't feel good, rework that list until you do feel good. Still not working? Jump back to attitude and re–center yourself. Once your emotional state is back on track, you'll be in alignment and ready to move forward toward your DGAs.

## Success Meditation #6: – New Behavior Generator

www.ChristopherCumby.com/SuccessMeditation

**JOURNAL NOTES:**

_____

_____

_____

_____

_____

_____

_____

_____

_____

_____

_____

_____

_____

_____

_____

_____

_____

**JOURNAL NOTES:**

_____

_____

_____

_____

_____

_____

_____

_____

_____

_____

_____

_____

_____

_____

_____

_____

_____

# 7 Accurate Thought: Inductive and Deductive Reasoning Attracts Success

> *"The accurate thinker deals with facts,*
> *regardless of how they affect his own interests,*
> *for he knows that ultimately*
> *this policy will bring him out on top,*
> *in full possession of the object of his definite*
> *chief aim in life."*
>
> Napoleon Hill

Now that you've digested the *Who A.R.E. You?* principle, let's continue the remarkable journey of developing your inner self and creating your ultimate success playbook. Understanding your deepest motivators and drivers lies at the heart of your personal development. To do so, you have to analyze, and then evaluate, the reasons why you do what you do. We all act with careful purpose, whether subconsciously or otherwise. There is no behavior or action we take without an initial thought that compels movement. So, our next lesson will explore inductive and deductive reasoning, often known as the foundation for our action or inaction.

## Understanding Your Reasons: Inductive vs. Deductive

Discovering the philosophy of reasoning in terms of inductive and deductive thinking opens your eyes to a new way of looking at things. The premise behind these techniques, if used correctly, is to view life either with a top–down (*deductive reasoning*) or bottom–up approach (*inductive reasoning*). Each vantage point offers distinct, beneficial opportunities to grow and develop, once you understand them.

> "You should carefully study the Art of Reasoning, as it is what most people are very deficient in, and I know few things more disagreeable than to argue, or even converse, with a man who has no idea of inductive and deductive philosophy."
>
> William John Wills

*Inductive reasoning* is a logical process in which multiple premises, all believed to true combine to reach a specific conclusion. Let's assume we visit a beach house and observe paintings of the ocean in each room we enter. By the time we reach the third or fourth room, we can safely assume that every remaining room will have an ocean painting. Another way to view this concept is to consider a group of dogs – your observations could lead you to conclude that because each of the dogs in the group barks, all dogs bark. While we haven't observed every dog in the world, we can conclude that because most dogs bark, all bark. Inductive reasoning is often used in applications that involve prediction, forecasting, or behavior. So based on past experience, we can predict that there will be an ocean painting in each room in that house and that all dogs bark. With inductive reasoning, the repetition of like objects, behaviors, etc. leads you to a conclusion about a larger grouping.

*Deductive reasoning* is a logical process where the general conclusion is based on multiple premises that are generally assumed to be true. Let's look at a few examples. In my family, because my wife runs, I cycle and our children swim and play soccer, we can conclude that the Cumby family is active. In terms of food, we can all agree that apples are a fruit, and all fruit grows on trees so all apples grow on trees. And if we know that Johnny has to be at work at 8:30 a.m. (and is never late), and his commute takes one hour, we can conclude that he leaves the house no later than 7:30 a.m. each day. Deductive reasoning lets us make conclusions about multiple items based on an assumption of truth for the group. We may not initially have the answer, but through deductive reasoning, we can come to a reliable hypothesis. With these examples, if a conclusion is wrong then the premise was faulty from the start. Fact checking becomes a very important part of your intellectual process.

Whether you use inductive or deductive reasoning, facts are crucial to getting the correct end result. You must learn to discern your observation (the premise) and find the truth through the process. Think about putting together a puzzle: you open the box, spread out the pieces and start categorizing. As you organize them by color and location, you begin to see the big picture. The same is true with reasoning. Each fact is a piece of the puzzle; as you group them together, you will arrive at specific and accurate conclusions and begin to see the big picture.

## The Value of Accurate Thinking

Both types of thinking, deductive and inductive, rely on accuracy. Organizing the pieces of your puzzle with greater accuracy will result in a higher likelihood of correct conclusions. We use both inductive and deductive reasoning; the major difference between the two is that inductive reasoning makes broad generalizations from specific observations while deductive reasoning starts out with a general statement and examines the possibilities to reach a specific logical conclusion. However, both cannot be used at the same time, or in conjunction with one another. It is like a "choose your own story" opportunity, you must select one path and remain with it until you reach your conclusion.

Neither one is better than the other, but inductive reasoning does allow you to observe more facts than possibilities. Meaning: your conclusion is based on ultimate truths. Again, consider a puzzle with its completed image in plain view. You'll be able to make specific conclusions because the end goal is right in front of you. Inductive reasoning is geared more toward the attainment of *truth*, which plays a pivotal role in becoming an accurate thinker. Accurate thinking uses facts over mere opinion, and it is based on the premise of securing a successful conclusion.

> "Have the courage to follow your heart and intuition. They somehow already know what you truly want to become. Everything else is secondary."
>
> Steve Jobs

In a perfect world, we would always have enough facts to inductively form a conclusion, but that's not always the case. We don't always have all the facts in front of us and are sometimes required to take a leap of faith.

Deductive reasoning plays an important role in, and is responsible for, your gut–feelings. You may find that facts you don't know may be assumed and then harnessed for accurate thinking. You can always look at possibilities using the deductive approach and apply faith to the outcome.

I believe that accurate thinking is something that most people could use to their benefit. We live in a world that leaves a lot of thought on the table, evidenced by our lack of cooperation and our remarkable practice of arguing about nearly every detail. If we chose to be more accurate in our thought processes, the world could be better positioned to focus on resolutions and not disagreements in thought.

Accurate thought was first introduced to me while studying the *Laws of Success in Sixteen Lessons* by Napoleon Hill. Hill suggests that accurate thinking is by far the most important concept to grasp in order to attain the true success you seek. It is also one of the most interesting and difficult concepts to teach, so reading this section more than once and taking notes may be helpful.

Essentially, accurate thinking is thinking on your own and becoming less reliant on the opinions of others. It ultimately connects to your spiritual being, or what many call your gut feeling or gut instinct. You've likely heard the phrase "trust your gut" – this is the idea behind accurate thinking. It is like the intersection of a strong and accurate mind with a focused and thoughtful inner compass. The process is independent of fear and requires you to abandon and dismantle your fears to ensure you are thinking in a lucid manner.

The first step to accurate thinking is: Once you truly *believe* that accurate thinking will improve your life, it will. Subsequently, you must also take action every day to support your training. Writing in your success playbook journal will keep you committed and accountable. This will be your greatest strength and will demolish fear within you that has kept you back from living the life you really want.

One of the greatest examples of accurate thought is Elon Musk. The CEO of Tesla, Musk has revolutionized the car industry, challenging the oil industry by building sleek, stylish, battery powered vehicles that have raised the bar within this industry. He is also the brain behind SpaceX, a company founded to "revolutionize space technology with the ultimate goal of enabling people to live on other planets." Musk wasn't content to simply facilitate space flights to the moon, like some competitors, he wanted to go further.

> "We do the missions that others think are impossible. We have goals that are absurdly ambitious by any reasonable standard, but we're going to make them happen."
>
> Elon Musk

Musk is a true pioneer of accurate thinking, as he believes he is destined to reach his goals through a dedicated and focused mindset. Few people have made the impossible possible like he has. In his world, everything is within reach and completely and utterly feasible. He lives in a world without limitations or boundaries. In his forties, Musk is now one of the most important thought leaders of our time.

*You must think differently* – not just differently from others, but differently from how you currently think.

Musk had *many* challenges, too many to list, but you can learn from his journey. He never gave up. He adapted to change. He relentlessly believed in his dreams. He sought facts to support his ideas. People laughed in his face, yet he keeps pushing the limits of man to the next level. He is an inspiration to us all. Maybe he will inspire you to be the next great thought leader.

## Turning Thought Into Action

So we have discussed the value found in inductive and deductive reasoning, and how we can use these approaches to create accurate thinking, but the question remains: How do we take these important ideas and manifest them into our own lives? Writing them down.

Let's outline the four steps for turning your thoughts into positive action.

The first step in visualizing your DGAs is putting pen to paper. This is the fun part. What do you really want? Write down your answers in the present tense – not in the past, not in the future. When you do this, keep your thoughts positive and focus on what you really want. Use phrases like *I choose...*(not *I need to*), *I have,...*(not *I will*), and *I am...*(not *I want*).

Now, take inventory of what is working against you. What emotions are holding you back from your life's goals? What emotions do you need to overcome these fears? What are your fears? What's relevant and important? This may be tough to face, but it is necessary for your growth.

There are really only two reasons you don't have what you want:

- *You are tuned in to your desires, dreams, and goals but have blocks and fears.*
- *You are just not tuned in at all.*

Most people I coach think there are tons of reasons why they don't have what they want. In fact, most are created based on their own limiting beliefs. This exercise should help you identify the things you need to change, and it should also teach you some new things about yourself.

The best part about journaling is that you'll just keep getting better. Soon you'll be able to write for hours if you choose. It took me some time to get in the habit of journaling, but it helped me better direct my thoughts toward my DGAs. It is important to focus on your *why* when journaling your DGAs. Your *why* creates a powerful energy and it gives your intentions the power and strength you need to succeed.

The third step is to identify your greatest strengths. Everyone has greatness inside them. Everyone has the ability to be truly remarkable and successful. Identify your strengths and you'll be one step closer to accessing more of your remarkable qualities. Write them down and you will remind yourself of the outstanding traits you already possess. Channeling your inner strengths is an influential way to strengthen your motivation and power you forward through obstacles.

The final step in becoming an accurate thinker is to find your bliss. Connect to what makes you the happiest in your life. Is it time with your family? Is it relaxing at the beach? Perhaps it is accomplishing your goals at work? Or maybe time spent with your dog? Happiness is the real pursuit of people who have achieved greatness in their lives. It is what will ultimately provide the peace we all seek inside. It is something that I know unequivocally has changed my life and allowed me to be successful. The same can be true for you.

## Visualizing an Invitation for Success

Surrounding yourself with like–minded people – those who contribute to your life in a positive way – supports the life you seek. So it is important for you to find what Napoleon Hill first coined as the *mastermind*, a group of people that bring knowledge you may not have to support a desire you imagine.

> "Imagination is more important than knowledge. Knowledge is limited. Imagination encircles the world."
>
> Albert Einstein

The mastermind principle has provided successful people like Elon Musk with an avenue to test ideas and gain new insights. It unlocks new ways to look at things and provides its members with the opportunity to learn from one another and their experiences. Building my companies required a mastermind, or people who had knowledge of what I needed to achieve my goals. In fact, masterminds have been around since the early evolution of commerce; history shows that people like Henry Ford relied on them to build their empires.

Unorganized knowledge is not power; it is potential power. Creating a mastermind that promotes a harmonious environment is the key. It is one of the most influential secrets to success, yet most people fail to utilize it in their own lives. Harnessing the thoughts of others is the way to achieve your greatest dreams. Create something in your mind and then find others to support its manifestation.

The mastermind is the culmination of using inductive and deductive reasoning skills. We all have goals – these goals are the end game. By assembling the pieces of the puzzle and forming thoughts that then become conclusions, we achieve our ultimate success. Accurate thinking is a powerful tool that supports our focus and helps us overcome obstacles in our path. We become more accurate thinkers when we write down our goals and review them daily. The pieces of this puzzle are spread out on the table. If we focus, the goal becomes clear and we can group our thoughts (or pieces) together to assemble the respective segments and reach our ultimate goals.

### Playbook Exercise 7:

Think about people who inspire you to take a chance, pursue your dreams and work to reach your goals.

- Write down the names of those people.

- List the things they accomplished that pique your interest.

- Now write down the qualities you admire in their personalities. Tenacity? Determination? Passion? Get specific. Get creative. Get inspired!

- How you can incorporate those inspirational traits into your life to bring you to new heights?

### Success Meditation #7: – Attracting Abundance

www.ChristopherCumby.com/SuccessMeditation

**JOURNAL NOTES:**

_____

_____

_____

_____

_____

_____

_____

_____

_____

_____

_____

_____

_____

_____

_____

_____

**JOURNAL NOTES:**

_____

_____

_____

_____

_____

_____

_____

_____

_____

_____

_____

_____

_____

_____

_____

_____

_____

_____

_____

# 8    The Power of Focus: Applying Faith in Action

> *"Faith is to believe what you do not see;*
> *the reward of this faith is to see what you believe."*
>
> Saint Augustine

Let's quickly review what we have covered so far. We have discussed the four pillars for building your success foundation, along with other lessons to help you find your success:

1. *Be Careful Who You Listen to*
2. *Keep Learning*
3. *Accept Change*
4. *Know Why You Want Something*

We learned that you are the creator of your life, and you, and only you, are responsible for what you have (or don't have). This concept separates you from the masses and strengthens your progression into an *accurate thinker*.

The *Who A.R.E. You?* principle brings clarity to your decision–making process, opening your eyes to who you really are and what you really want. It brings greater clarity and more focused direction to your life's journey.

Finally, we learned about accurate thought. The goal is to arm you with a new technique to focus your attention on important and relevant information for the purpose of achieving your chief aim in life.

Now we arrive at the power of *focus*. This is an area that most people recognize and understand, but have never mastered. In this chapter, we will discover the power of mastery and how to use focus to achieve your DGAs.

> "That's been one of my mantras – focus and simplicity.
> Simple can be harder than complex:
> You have to work hard to get your thinking clean,
> to make it simple.
> But, it's worth it in the end because once you get there,
> you can move mountains."
>
> Steve Jobs

And move mountains he did. Steve Jobs was relentlessly focused on his goal, revolutionizing the way the world communicates. Jobs spoke of simplicity and access, both of which he gave to the world with innovations such as the iPod, iPhone and FaceTime. In fact, I can attest to this simplicity as I watched my then eighteen–month–old son use an iPad before he fully knew his ABCs. Now that's *success*!

> "Successful people maintain a positive focus in life no matter what is going on around them. They stay focused on their past successes rather than their past failures, and on the next action steps they need to take to get them closer to the fulfillment of their goals rather than all the other distractions that life presents to them."
>
> Jack Canfield

The power of focus lies in examining your life experiences for the lessons they provide you.

Focus is like a hammer striking a nail into place. Carpenters need hammers to effectively accomplish their jobs. When focused, that tool can hammer enough nails to build a house. For you, focus will be your hammer, a common tool you'll use more than anything else.

Focus eliminates the irrelevant things that appear in life. It is a key component to becoming an accurate thinker. When you allow your attention to drift, you lose the intensity necessary to accomplish your goals – instead filling your mind with unimportant information.

*Focus and don't be overwhelmed by the noise.*

When I began working in the energy industry, my success depended on my proven sales skills. As my sales grew, so did my profile and companies impressed by my skill set began recruiting me. These companies made some very attractive offers, but I opted to follow my mentor's advice and stay focused on the task at hand, my current business. The advice paid off and my income grew ten times over the course of the following 18 months.

The lesson to learn is you will get closer to the desired positive outcome, even through failure. With a negative result, you'll learn what not to do. Eventually any shortcomings will create enough momentum to teach you lessons about reaching your goals. Just take Thomas Edison – he failed countless times before the light bulb *went off* in his head.

Focusing is the act of bestowing your concentration on one singular goal. The mind is enormously powerful, and when applied directly it can accomplish phenomenal outcomes. Your environment not only plays an important part in success, it's also is crucial for focused attention. Personally, I require a place that stimulates my creativity when I write; it allows greater focus and nurtures my thoughts. Being around water allows me to better channel my energy into a focused state, much like a laser beam concentrates light into a very specific location.

Using the power of focus allows you to leap into a zone of perfection. It allows you to connect to your thoughts and be creative with their outcomes. There are several ways to build this perfect environment, and we will discuss the most powerful ones near the end of this chapter.

## Creating Dominant Thought Patterns

Focus is like a small seed that has to be nurtured in a rich, viable environment. One of the best ways to support that growth is by creating dominant thought patterns.

*You are what you think about most of the time.* So, creating a life filled with dominant thought patterns will soon have your life mirroring your thoughts.

Dominant thoughts are responsible for most of your current life. The good news is you can focus your attention to create new outcomes, or paradigms, anytime. A paradigm is a distinct set of ideas or thought patterns. We all have paradigms, whether we think about them or not. In fact, some of these paradigms are totally subconscious; but they're not constant. We have the ability to change them all.

A paradigm shift takes focus – a strong ability to assess your current state and recognize the energy you are giving to areas that don't serve your chief aim, or purpose. You must find your purpose, and when you do, you must concentrate your thoughts solely on it. The art of accurate thinking will help you determine what is relevant to this purpose, aiding you in the separation of helpful thoughts from harmful ones. When you master this skill, your reality will change. You won't struggle to manifest what you desire and you won't worry about when it will actually happen.

Becoming fearless in the pursuit of your chief aim means controlling your way of thinking. There will be no negative thought patterns. No doubts. No fears. In doing so, you'll find your outlook is now positive and supportive. In fact, you'll find confidence in your newfound ability, and fear will be eliminated from your thoughts.

Fear is made up. It is inside your head. It is the result of a lack of faith. We let fear creep into our lives and chew away at us. Don't allow that to happen! Instead, apply faith and manifest a new reality, one that is inspiring, uplifting and your own.

Learning how to swim can be very scary and simply "jumping in" is not the best way to learn. Most of us are taught to start in the shallow area or use a flotation device. From there we slowly learn to dunk our head, hold our breath, move our arms and legs and swim short distances, with some assistance. With repetition and practice, we swim with more confidence. Soon we are fearless swimmers.

Being fearless in life is similar: go slow, adapt to situations and learn small things that can help you hold on. As you practice and gain confidence, you will be a fearless risk taker, going after the things you want.

## Applied Faith: Manifesting Your Reality

If fear is the venom, then faith is your antidote. Faith is not just religion, although religion does rely heavily on faith. Faith is energy, or a frequency, a powerful force permeating our universe. Faith is your ability to accept something without any physical evidence of its existence. Faith has no physical presence; it is a feeling that lies within each of us. To strengthen your faith, you must give up fearful thinking because fear cannot survive in faith.

When I was nine, the school system convinced my parents to place me in a special education class. I was mortified, embarrassed and felt defeated. Looking back, it was, surprisingly, a blessing in disguise. In that special education class, I was free to explore; there was less structure than the "normal" classes so I focused my attention on science and art. These subjects fascinated me and really sparked my curiosity. I fell in love with the teachings of people like Albert Einstein and Pablo Picasso; they became my heroes. I read about how *they* used faith to break boundaries within their lives and that encouraged me to do the same.

I believe our lives are designed by how we think and fueled by how we feel. I knew, even at that young age, that I was responsible for everything my future held. After four years of being in special education, I asked to take an aptitude test to determine my readiness for "normal" classes. I aced them – shocking everyone, except me, with those results. I went on to high school, became an A student and graduated with honors. I did all this by applying faith to my thoughts and outcomes.

So what is applied faith?

> "Applied faith is your greatest asset.
> Simply put, it is the mental attitude wherein you may clear your mind of all fears and doubts and direct it to the attainment of whatever you desire in life."
>
> Napoleon Hill

With my special education experience, it was something I did without even realizing it. I developed a positive attitude, and with the freedom to think, my desire to learn helped me escape the label others had given me: special.

And if I can do that, so can you.

Some of my favorite mentors from my imaginary council applied faith as well. Abraham Lincoln used applied faith to enact the Emancipation Proclamation of 1863, despite many people believing it to be impossible. He harnessed energy through his positive mindset; never allowing negative energy to destroy what he firmly believed was possible. It is a great lesson in believing in your dream; Lincoln's dream changed the world.

Oprah Winfrey is another example of someone accomplishing a great deal through applied faith. Oprah had a challenging upbringing. She grew up with very little; she suffered abuse as a child; and became pregnant as a teenager. Yet she overcame that adversity and went after her dreams with determination and confidence. She pioneered an industry – transitioning from a broadcast journalist to being named the Queen of All Media. She introduced new concept of daytime talk show focusing on spirituality, self–help, and self–improvement. Oprah's life experience drove her and inspired her commitment to philanthropy. She applied faith. Oprah did not simply envision and believe what she wanted; she also took action. This principle applies to everything in our universe. Nothing stands still. Your dreams, like everything else in this universe, require energy. Keep your dreams in motion!

Be part of the less crowded group. Take action every day and apply faith to those actions. You will accomplish whatever you want if you do not give up.

Many stumble into faith through hardship and curiosity. And many lose that faith just as easily. It may seem elusive initially, but trusting your DGAs, being confident and eliminating fear will allow faith to make your dreams a reality.

> "There are basically two types of people. People who accomplish things, and people who claim to have accomplished things. The first group is less crowded."
>
> Mark Twain

Your environment is yours to create, and it will be different for everyone, the key is to journal and unlock what is important for you to thrive. Here is a hint, nature is a good place to start, the beach, and the forest can do wonders for you.

**Playbook Exercise 8:**

There are two parts to this chapter's exercise.

1. Let's create a roadmap, much like taking a trip from Point A to Point B. Determine where you are (Point A), this will provide clarity for plotting the necessary route to get to your goal (Point B). List some stopping points along your route. This will give you measurable milestones and feasible mini–goals along the way. They also lessen your risk of going in the wrong direction, helping you stay focused. These stopping points will hold you accountable, and when you stay on track, your chances of arriving at your goal increase exponentially.

   An example: Mason enjoys woodworking in his free time. He would like to eventually make this his full time career. Point A: Woodworking on evenings and weekends in addition to his full time job. Point B: Quitting his full time job and replacing that income with revenue from his custom woodworking business. What are some feasible stopping points for Mason? He'll need to grow his business, should he advertise? Should he photograph his work? Should he have current clients provide testimonials? Can he take classes to expand his knowledge of woodworking techniques? Does he use social media?

   Let this example serve as an outline for your own roadmap.

2. Let's take a few moments and find a quiet place to take inventory of your faith.

   - Where would you like to apply your faith?
   - What is it you really want?

   Stop and really think about it. Go slow, breathe deeply and let your thoughts guide you. Smile knowing that you are in control and that you can accomplish this. You are already applying faith to ensure no amount of fear stops you in your tracks.

**Success Meditation #8: – Future Pacing**

www.ChristopherCumby.com/SuccessMeditation

**JOURNAL NOTES:**

_____

_____

_____

_____

_____

_____

_____

_____

_____

_____

_____

_____

_____

_____

_____

_____

_____

_____

## JOURNAL NOTES:

# 9  Dominating Your Thoughts:
It's Your Thinking That Makes It So

> *"You are now, and you do become, what you think about."*
>
> Earl Nightingale

In the previous chapter, we learned the power of focus. In this chapter, we will explore how thought creates that power. Thought is often overlooked by the masses, since most of us were never taught the techniques or tools to drive our lives with determination. That is about to change.

To understand how thinking makes it so, we need to understand the differences and similarities between accurate thought and dominant thought. Even though dominant and accurate thoughts support each other, it is important to realize their unique strengths and distinctions.

- *Dominant thought* is the ability to concentrate your focus on a specific thought, goal, or endeavor.

- *Accurate thought* is the ability to find facts to support your goals and endeavors.

Dominant thoughts are responsible for your entire life so far. In fact, your most dominant thoughts control your outcomes and have resulted in your current experience. According to the law of attraction, popularized by Esther and Jerry Hicks, in order to create specific dominant thoughts, you must **focus your attention for 68 seconds** and do this until the thought permeates the subconscious mind and becomes constant. As the Hicks say, *"If you manage to stay purely focused upon any thought for as little as 68 seconds, the vibration is powerful enough that its manifestation begins."*[1]

---

1    www.healyourlife.com/got-68-seconds

> "Accurate thought involves two fundamentals which all who indulge in it must observe.
> First, to think accurately you must separate facts from mere information. There is much 'information' available to you that is not based upon facts.
> Second, you must separate facts into two classes; namely, the important and the unimportant, or, the relevant and the irrelevant.
> Only by doing so can you think clearly."[2]
>
> Napoleon Hill

As we've discussed, we all have a hypnotic rhythm to our day based on our habitual thoughts, actions, and vibrations. To create new habits, we must consciously pay attention. Dominant thought relies on the subconscious mind; accurate thought relies on the conscious mind. Blending the two is a powerful way to direct your life and attain your DGAs.

## Dominate Your Thoughts

To reap the benefits of dominant thought, you must first learn how to control what you think about. It helps to follow these four steps to ensure you are on the right path.

1. Tune into your internal dialogue

2. Identify your blocks and limiting beliefs

3. Direct your awareness and energy

4. Accomplishing it all

## Tune Into Your Internal Dialogue

You are responsible for everything that has happened, is happening, and is going to happen in your life. Don't fear this; embrace it.

---

2    www.archive.org/details/Law_Of_Success_in_16_Lessons

The first step to strengthening this attribute is to pay attention to your inner dialogue, or your *self–talk*. This is something we all do, whether we are conscious of it or not. We all have components inside us: one that is ego/mind and one that is connected on a deeper level to the soul, the one I like to call my *other–self*.

We often have inner dialogues in our head between our ego/mind and our other–self, both consciously and subconsciously. Until you become aware of this *other–self*, this counterpart to your ego, you may never find your true calling in life.

Self–talk is one of the most important attributes of a truly successful person. Tune into your *other self*. Tune out the ego. Listen to your internal dialogue. You will get better at controlling your outcomes and listening to your soul for answers.

## Identify Your Blocks and Limiting Beliefs

When you study your inner dialogue, you'll discover your blocks and limiting beliefs. You will know what is holding you back. Once you know what they are, you can dissect them. You can take them apart piece by piece. You can let go of these assumptions, and begin to make your own truths.

## Direct Your Awareness and Energy

> "What you seek, seeks you."
>
> Rumi

You already know what happens to you is attracted through your vibration and frequency. What you give off, through your thoughts and feelings, connects you to similar thoughts and feelings. Directing your awareness and energy, either consciously or unconsciously, will lead you to a more conscious level of creativity. Your success playbook journal will help get you there.

## Accomplishing It All

Accomplishment through thought direction is the pathway to true success. Creating the life you want is entirely based on setting yourself up to win. What does that mean? Accomplishments are made by creating a blueprint or plan; a step–by–step approach to goal setting. Break down your life goals into smaller, manageable steps.

Setting and achieving little goals sets up a winning outcome every day. You begin creating a frequency of accomplishment, and accomplishment is a great feeling. Breaking goals down into smaller tasks is guaranteed to create a habit of success. Your outlook stays positive because these small steps are attainable, not overwhelming. As you accomplish each one, you'll realize your progress toward your goal. You'll see just how far you've come and how much you are capable of achieving.

Building success in your life requires patience, but perhaps most importantly it requires you to know why you want something. Understand that taking small steps each day with a consistent effort will lead you to where you want to be. I like to remind myself to *"walk as far as I can see and I will see a little further."*

## It's Your Thinking That Makes It So

> "Our life always expresses the result of our dominant thoughts."
>
> Soren Kierkegaard

To better understand the power of dominant thought, let's look at the lives, and successes, of some incredible thinkers – people who know that *thinking makes it so.*

Sara Blakely, the creator of Spanx Inc., used dominant thought to create a successful business. Spanx was created in the late 1990s during Sara's career in fax sales. She was working in the heat and humidity and was desperately looking for solution to her work attire that provided the slimming properties of traditional pantyhose and didn't cover her toes. Frustrated by a lack of bodyshaping products, Sara decided to make her own. She worked tirelessly, in her free time, designing and testing styles. Finally, pleased with her final product, she took samples to area department stores and sold them on the concept of Spanx. She has expanded her product line over the course of two decades, making Spanx the global leader in shapewear.

Early on, Sara realized the hosiery industry had been doing the same thing for decades with no change. By customizing her product offerings and developing different sizes and shapes, Sara revolutionized an industry.

Why was Sara was so successful? First, she found a need that wasn't being met. She wanted the silhouette that pantyhose provided but she wanted it to stop at the ankle so she could wear open toed shoes. Because our brains are wired to solve problems, hers went to work to create a solution. Sara thought about this frequently (it was *dominant* in her thoughts). She studied the undergarment industry, she tested ideas with friends and family and over time, her idea turned into a multi–million dollar success story.

That is the power of dominant thinking. Combining this with accurate thoughts (finding *facts* to support her idea through *research*), Sara was able to move mountains in an industry that had been stagnant for decades. Spanx is a great example of using the mind to solve challenges and come up with solutions. Sara's persistent imagination created a product that so many people can benefit from today and she disrupted an industry along the way.

Brett Toskan is another dominant thinker; an inspiring business owner and young COO who runs a national sales–focused experiential marketing firm, Kognitive Marketing. Brett and I became friends while living in Toronto, and through many great discussions I learned how he created his successful company from scratch.

Brett attributes a portion of his success to his work ethic and determination, values instilled in him by his grandparents who immigrated to Canada with limited resources, working as farmers until settling in Toronto. Their determination and commitment to hard work laid the groundwork for their children's, and grandchildren's, success. Brett's uncle, Frank Toskan, co–created MAC cosmetics and made it a success with of the help of his immediate family. Both Frank Toskan and Victor Casale, lead chemist and another uncle, were instrumental in teaching Brett through his early years. He attributes his business poise and acumen to the mentorship and support they continue to provide him.

Brett also appreciates his aunt, Julie Toskan–Casale, for inspiring his positive thinking and philanthropic outlook. While also an integral part of the success of MAC, she is now the president of Toskan Casale Foundation and focuses her energy into its Youth and Philanthropy Initiative, a program she created, launched, and implemented into secondary schools in Canada, the United Kingdom, and New York City. This initiative helps youth research and become aware of community–based social service issues and the charities that support them. With help from the foundation, the YPI program empowers students by awarding the best student presentation in each participating school with a financial grant to the charity researched.

Brett believes in the power of focus and determination. He attributes his success to being completely obsessed with Kognitive Marketing's growth, development, and innovation, which ultimately led to the business receiving the award for the fastest–growing marketing company in Canada, the 2014 *Canadian Business* Profit500 award.

Another inspiring thinker, and close friend, is Gary Green, the youngest coach in National Hockey League (NHL) history. Although he excelled on the ice, his connection to the NHL would begin with coaching. He coached a very successful minor league team, winning the league's prestigious Coach of the Year award before becoming the head coach of the Washington Capitals at age 26.

Gary set his goal of becoming a coach in the NHL, and dominated his thoughts with achieving this dream. He loves hockey and is one of the first to successfully transition from NHL alumni to television broadcaster.

Gary was accurate in the pursuit of his dreams. His secret to success is you must love and be passionate about what you do. Loving his career is what allowed Gary to be one of the most memorable coaches and broadcasters in NHL history.

There are common traits among these successful individuals: they mentored with people they admired and trusted, they had a clear focus, and they dominated their thoughts with accuracy. These secrets lie in plain sight. There is nothing complicated about success – your thoughts are what drive it.

And it isn't just successful people demonstrating the power of dominant thought – the scientific community is testing its impact as well. According to an article in *Scientific American*:

*"We can choose to adopt a mindset that improves creativity [...]People who think of categories as flexible and actively focus on the novel aspects of the environment become more creative."[3]*

> "If I have the belief that I can do it, I shall surely acquire the capacity to do it even if I may not have it at the beginning."
>
> Mahatma Gandhi

This newfound ability of becoming an accurate thinker and dominating your thoughts will attract what you seek. We all have the ability to reach our DGAs by tuning in to our dominant, accurate thoughts and using them to create our best selves.

Take what you have learned in this chapter and apply it to your life. Practice dominant and accurate thought so you can better achieve your DGAs. It will involve hard work, but if you believe in yourself, success will come.

*Find your magnificent obsession and be persistent with every thought that supports its manifestation.*

---

3       www.scientificamerican.com/article/your-thoughts-can-release-abilities-beyond-normal-limits/

**Playbook Exercise 9:**

In your journal answer the following questions. Go slowly, ponder the questions, and feel your answers.

- What is it you want?

- Why do you want it?

- What feeling do you want when you get what you want?

- What is missing from your life now?

- What do you need and why do you need it?

**Success Meditation #9: – Ego Strengthening**

www.ChristopherCumby.com/SuccessMeditation

**JOURNAL NOTES:**

_____

_____

_____

_____

_____

_____

_____

_____

_____

_____

_____

_____

_____

_____

_____

_____

_____

_____

**JOURNAL NOTES:**

# 10 The Path to Your Goals: Fear Indecision, Not Wrong Decisions

You have invested a fair amount of time into reading this book and learning its lessons. It's now to time to ask yourself:

*Why are you reading this book?*

Did you answer that question? Many just keep reading. Maybe you are excited to learn more so you kept going. Or maybe we are so accustomed to speeding through life that we forget to slow down. And that's a lesson we all need to put into practice: take the time to think.

So why *are* you reading this book?

Now that you've taken a minute, or five, to think about this question, what did you discover? What are you looking for? What have you found? Have you had any "a–ha!" moments?

This exercise is designed to help you gain control of your ego/mind. It serves as a reminder that you don't have to rush through things. We live in a fast world, make the time to stop and contemplate.

## The Role of Indecision

Remember this adage:

> "Successful people make decisions quickly
> and change their minds slowly,
> while unsuccessful people change their minds
> often and never make a decision."

Asking better questions in life will lead to more confidence in following your internal guidance system, or *gut feeling*. Tapping into this intuition will enable you to be more decisive.

Bob Proctor, one of my mentors, says:

"There is a single mental move you can make
which, in a millisecond,
will solve enormous problems for you.
It has the potential to improve almost
any personal or business situation
you will ever encounter
...and it could literally propel you
down the path to incredible success.
We have a name for this magic mental activity
...it is called decision.
Decisions, or the lack of them,
are responsible for the breaking or
making of many a career."

To understand the importance of decisions, we must examine indecision. What is indecision? Why are so many people indecisive in their lives? The answer is simple – they fear the unknown and are not skilled in making decisions. The good new is decision–making is a skill you can develop and master.

Many people lack clarity in their decision–making. With indecision, choices are left open, creating more uncertainty. Allowing this indecision to creep in and take control will perpetuate a cycle of fear–driven actions that lead to inaction. There's no action. There's no movement. There's no growth.

## Why Any Decision is Better than Indecision

Years ago, several business partners and I were in the process of selling our company. We were indecisive on which sales model we should implement after we merged into a larger organization. We waffled on how to structure the company post–merger and the results were disappointing, with our team being dismantled shortly after the deal was signed. Being indecisive about the direction our specific business unit should take ruined our business.

Leaving a company you built isn't easy; it's downright painful. So how did I turn it around? One day I decided I would no longer accept my current reality as my truth. In that moment, I decided to follow my dream by using my strengths and changing my view of the world around me.

Since then, I have perfected the art of decision–making. I do not waver in the face of decision. Instead, I make them quickly and change my mind slowly.

## The Value of Wrong Decisions

What is the difference between indecision and wrong decision?

Indecision holds you back in life. It consumes you with fear, doubt and the "what if?" cycle. Decide. Act. Move forward.

> "Knowledge comes from learning, and wisdom comes from living."
>
> Anthony Douglas Williams

Wrong decisions are still decisions and should be viewed positively as long as you learn from them. Live and learn to make decisions. You won't always make the best one, but it *will* lead you to where you need to go. The key is not to let it defeat you.

*Trust that with every decision you make it will guide you to the next one, and with each turn in life, as long as you focus your attention on what you really want, you will arrive just in time.*

Failure is simply a temporary defeat. Learn from your mistakes. Map out what you will do differently next time. Then let it go. Failures will take place. Wrong decisions will be made. They are lessons for getting it right in the future.

So go ahead and just make a decision. Even if it doesn't produce the results you are hoping for, it will certainly push you farther than not deciding at all.

### The Art of Decision Making

Many people don't know how to make a decision. They ponder thoughts but don't move ahead due to fear of making the wrong decision. Sound familiar? More than 95 percent of people in the world never realize their goals because they are unable to make a decision and move toward their dreams. They allow imaginary defeat and criticism to overtake their minds, but this can be avoided.

The Decision–Making Formula is designed to give you more confidence when faced with a decision. It is a way to strengthen your resolve when fear and doubt start to cloud your choices.

## The Decision–Making Formula

### Alignment + Time + Investment + Accepting the Outcome = SUCCESS

**Alignment:**   Ensuring the desire you are trying to achieve aligns with your true self.

1. Do you believe you can attain this?
2. Does this excite you?
3. Does this align with your values?
4. Are you willing to stay teachable and learn?
5. Are you willing to accept change where necessary?

**Time:**   Allowing the time to learn and make the changes necessary for attainment of your goals. Decide how long you think it will take; then add 50 percent more time.

**Investment**: Understanding the investment of money and/or time for attainment. Determine how much of an investment you will have to make; then add 50 percent more.

**Accepting the**
**Outcome**: Have you addressed the end result of failure? Can you live with that outcome? Have you addressed the end result of success? How will you feel upon achievement? Would this make you happy?

This simple formula is missing in most people's lives. They simply don't take the time to understand the importance of decision–making and as a result, they fall short of their DGAs. Don't let this happen to you.

You have the ability to attain anything you want in life. There is opportunity in every dream – look around and witness this for yourself. Pay attention. The prosperity you seek is within your ability, if only you can learn and change – it is as simple as that.

Practice the Decision–Making Formula whenever you are faced with an important decision. It will simplify the way you view the situation.

## Start Deciding

This chapter has shown you the positive power of decision–making and the dangers of indecision. You are ready to accept wrong decisions as learning lessons and move forward with your life. You are ready to let go of fear and uncertainty and embrace decisiveness. You are ready to slow down and take the time needed to answer important questions. As a result, you will receive better answers.

Remember to go slow. This is not a race; this is your life. You can live it the way you want. Ask better questions, understand the answers you receive, seek out facts and dismiss opinions. The path to becoming an accurate and decisive thinker is already underway.

"If you wish to achieve
worthwhile things
in your personal and career life,
you must become
a worthwhile person
in your own
self—development."

Brian Tracy

This is your life, live it the way you want!

**Playbook Exercise 10:**

Let's apply the Decision–Making Formula to one of your goals.

Write down your goal and answer the following questions:

**Alignment:**

1. Do you believe you can attain this goal?
2. Does it excite you?
3. Does it align with your values?
4. Are you willing to be teachable and learn?
5. Are you willing to accept change where necessary?

**Time:**

Define how much time you'll need to reach this goal (and add 50 percent more).

**Investment:**

Determine how much time and/or money you'll need to invest in your goal, and add 50 percent more.

**Accepting the Outcome:**

- What will happen if you fail?
- Can you live with that outcome?
- What will happen if you succeed?
- How will you feel when you achieve this goal?
- Would this make you happy?

**Success Meditation #10: – Mind Flow**

www.ChristopherCumby.com/SuccessMeditation

**JOURNAL NOTES:**

_____

_____

_____

_____

_____

_____

_____

_____

_____

_____

_____

_____

_____

_____

_____

_____

_____

**JOURNAL NOTES:**

# 11 Understand Your Belief System: Desire + Awareness = Results

Understanding our belief system is crucial to positive transformation. To fully comprehend the power of belief, we have to know how beliefs originate. Being aware of how our beliefs are developed gives us the opportunity to shape our own belief system and gain control over our lives. We have the ability to control what and whom we believe in. Let's look at some people whose belief systems inspired greatness in our world.

## Belief That Inspires

> "There is no passion to be found playing small –
> in settling for a life that is less than the one
> you are capable of living."
>
> Nelson Mandela

Nelson Mandela's beliefs were shaped from a very young age. As a child, he dreamed of making a contribution to his country by helping alleviate the struggles of his community. He wanted to help people improve their lives in a positive manner. He dreamed of peace, as he saw far too much conflict and animosity growing up. He knew what he didn't want, so he identified and focused on what he did want.

In a country plagued by disease and apartheid, Mandela fought for the equality of all people. He developed a strong sense of hope that one day his life experience would bring change.

This didn't come without a cost. Mandela spent almost three decades in prison for treason. But Mandela believed in his purpose, and the solitude he endured in prison allowed him to find an inner peace that would resonate with the outside world.

In 1993, Nelson Mandela was awarded the Nobel Peace Prize for his work toward the peaceful termination of apartheid and for laying the foundation for a new democratic South Africa. Mandela first found inner peace and when he shared it, his childhood dream was realized.

Mandela's story is spectacular. It showed the world that anything is possible as long as you believe.

Another story of hope and courage is that of Terry Fox. At the age of 19, he was diagnosed with a form of cancer called osteosarcoma that resulted in the amputation of his right leg. Fox was an athlete and had competed in multiple sports, but developed a passion for long-distance running. He had a positive attitude that was unwavering and it sparked his decision to travel across his native Canada, on foot, to raise funds and awareness for cancer research.

Fox set a goal to raise $24 million by getting one dollar from each Canadian. His marathon of hope is still active today and has raised more than $600 million towards cancer research, far exceeding his original goal.

Terry Fox had an unshakable belief system. He was persistent and very competitive, and those traits drove him to overcome the adversity he would later face. He never allowed cancer to get in the way of his goals.

Fox may not have beat cancer himself, but his actions raised money to advance cancer research and care for millions of Canadians battling this disease. His determination in his beliefs helped and inspired countless people around the world.

So what did Mandela and Fox have in common?

The challenges they faced in life inspired them to make a difference for others with similar circumstances. Their backgrounds and environments were completely different, yet their global impact is still felt, celebrated and reciprocated years after their passing. They contributed greatly to our society by offering hope and encouragement in bleak situations and believing that changes could be made.

*Knowingness* comes from a sense of oneness. It has no fixed position of opinion; instead, it is a feeling that all is connected. When you have *knowingness* there is no need to convince anyone of anything. Inside you feel it – you sense the purpose and do not need to defend your position. You simply have a state of acceptance, complete understanding, and certainty.

I believe both Mandela and Fox had an inner knowingness about their destiny. They followed an internal drive that they did not need to defend. They were certain of what they knew, what they believed and understood the why behind their life experiences.

You too have an *inner knowingness* within you. Once you commit to something and strongly believe you can attain it, the knowingness inside will take over. The universe places the right people, events, circumstances and places in your path. You will experience an *inner knowingness* you will follow.

## Understanding Why You Think the Way You Think

Our brains are fascinating. They have the capacity to house billions of data points and with each thought create new neuro–pathways. You think the way you do because of the dominant thought patterns you have formed over time. You have created everything that has happened, is happening, and will happen. Your inner feelings vibrate and send signals to your brain, creating thoughts, and each thought then gets associated with the vibration (negative or positive). This connection to vibration is why all the gurus talk about positive thought – because you have the power to *feel good*. Science tells us that a human being pays ten times more attention to the negative attributes of life than the positive attributes. But we don't have to spend that much time focused on negativity – we can *choose* positivity. We just need to retrain the brain.

Belief systems are a set of rules your brain has associated with outcomes that you may have learned, experienced, and/or made up. Fear is one of those things. We avoid things that hurt our ego/mind.

In fact, the ego encourages us to flee when the going gets tough but you don't have to run from your fear.

You overcome fear when you learn there are really no failures in life. All setbacks are temporary. With fear removed, your *inner knowingness* that you can attain anything you imagine, accept as truth, or fully believe begins to take root. There is power in faith. Look inside yourself and start a new belief. Accept it, embrace it and practice it daily. You will access your capacity to manifest greatness.

Social heredity is defined as the things you have learned from the time you were in the womb until the present day. Information is passed down through evolution, from generation to generation. According to Herbert William Conn, the author of *Social Heredity and Social Environment, The Other Side of Eugenics*, the human race is a culmination of evolutionary changes. This means we are born with embedded characteristics passed down through generations of our family. We are subject to the environmental influence of our families and the social settings of our upbringing. This is why so many people have a hard time breaking free from their fears and doubts. They are ingrained.

You can change this. Old patterns and habits may linger but you can rewire your thought patterns to avoid their influence. Let me put it another way: If a road stopped being used, it would eventually be overrun by vegetation and the pavement would crumble. Your mind works the same way. When you reconfigure your same train of thought, that old, negative neuro–pathway is no longer used.

Tony Robbins says it best:

> "Progress equals happiness."

As human beings, progress is in our DNA. We are meant to grow and learn. We are destined for greatness, and all we need to do to access this incredible magic is retrain our brains.

## Break Free of Old Habits to Create New Ones

I am going to use the remainder of this chapter to teach you *dream building*.

Dream building is a basic technique that helps you imagine all the possibilities available to you. Like anything new, it can be a little intimidating initially, but keep moving forward. With practice, you will not only create an impressive list of dreams, you'll begin to grow the list into the *Journal of a Thousand Dreams*.

Yes …a thousand. That number may seem extreme, at first, but if you limit your dreams and have a small list, you may get discouraged when one or more don't happen. But if you have many DGAs, the universe will allow them to find you.

Dream building also has another element to it, and that is the tangible element. Physically touching a DGA is the best way for you to feel what it would be like to have it.

A great example is a luxury car. If you went and sat in it, test drove it, and experienced the new car smell, you're activating your senses. When your senses are activated, and you're able to visualize getting this car, you're motivated to take action. This is when dream boards, visualization and meditation get incorporated into your dream building. When all practiced together, it is only a matter of time before you actualize your goals.

Another example highlights the power of compounding.

Imagine your fridge is on the fritz and it's time for a new one. You'll spend time researching until you find one that will do the trick. But let's take it further. What if you look at the entire appliance package? What if you just renovate your entire kitchen along with that new fridge and other appliances? Or better still, how about a new house with a brand–new kitchen and top–of–the–line appliances?

That's compounding and how it fits into your *dream building*.

If you were to attain any one of the goals on your list, would you be happy? Of course you would, so why limit them to a small list? That is the point of the Journal of a Thousand Dreams – the more you have, the more likely the universe will align and put them in front of you. Once you attain one, you'll raise your vibration and frequency, which in turn will attract more of your goals.

Dream building is what sets the successful apart from the unsuccessful. It is a stronger, more effective way to reach your DGAs.

Another element of setting your dreams and desires into motion is the unique concept of open time frames, and being less specific.

What does that mean?

Without a time frame, I knew I wouldn't be discouraged if a goal took longer than expected. Whenever it happened, I would be thrilled. Being non–specific may be the most interesting way to attain what you want. It requires you to be open and fluid, like water. Being non–specific in this regard is the best way to have peace within while working towards your DGAs.

When I learned that I could be general in setting my goals, knowing that their attainment would be faster, I was hooked. I set no time frame to them, because whenever they happened I would be equally happy. This way you don't get discouraged if a goal takes longer than others.

To better illustrate, here is another example. Let's set a goal of wanting a new house. You would create a list of everything you'd like in the house and all the things it would provide. Then you would search for homes and schedule tours. This would enable you to physically touch the homes and visualize yourself in them. Then, as you hone in on the specific house you want, you would let go of that house. Why? There may be several others who want that house as well.

This is where the power of non—specificity comes into play. If there were an equal or even better house for you, would you be happy with that? Probably. So you continue to focus on the attributes and features of the home you want, but trust that they are available in several different homes you have yet to see.

Having an open, fluid approach to possible outcomes ensures that disappointment and negativity don't drag you down. If someone else got the house, this sad vibration would just attract more discouragement. Learning to flow and allowing your goals to come to you, you'll find you're less concerned about their immediate attainment. Trust that your DGAs are attainable and they will come to you when you're ready.

With practice, your DGAs will reach a thousand, and when they do, you'll look at your life differently.

## Start Building

> "People rarely succeed unless they have fun in what they are doing."
>
> Dale Carnegie

Understanding our belief systems is crucial to living the life we desire. This chapter has provided you with the information you need to understand the factors and influences that affect your beliefs, and the techniques you can use to change them. There is no reason to remain stuck in negative belief patterns that don't align with your vision. Take the time to create an inner knowingness so you can lead yourself down the right path. Practice dream building regularly, and you'll attract new levels of success.

**Playbook Exercise 11:**

Draw a vertical line down the middle of a blank page in your playbook. On the left, write down the things you want. On the right, write down the things you love.

How many things did you write in the left column, the things you want? Now review it, and add more. This may take a few tries, because you may be limiting yourself, even in your dreams. Don't limit yourself.

How many things did you write on the right–hand side, the things you love? No matter how many you listed, get creative and write more. The key is to list even your wildest, most idealistic dreams and loves – all of them. So dig deep.

Let's look at your love list. Is there anything there that is more of a like? Ask yourself: Do I love that or simply want it? Armed with those answers, edit your list.

Do you need to make changes to your list? Do you still love lots of things or just a few? It is okay either way. As you learn more about dream building, you will get better and better with this exercise.

Now let's look at your want list and answer the following questions:

- Have you physically touched this want?
- Have you experienced this want in any way?
- Why do you want it?
- What feeling does this want give you?
- Why do you want that feeling?
- When you achieve this want, will you still want it?

Revisit your wants and loves periodically and reassess what you're striving to achieve.

**Success Meditation #11: – Confidence**

www.ChristopherCumby.com/SuccessMeditation

**JOURNAL NOTES:**

_____

_____

_____

_____

_____

_____

_____

_____

_____

_____

_____

_____

_____

_____

_____

_____

_____

**JOURNAL NOTES:**

_____

_____

_____

_____

_____

_____

_____

_____

_____

_____

_____

_____

_____

_____

_____

_____

_____

# 12 Creating Positive Habits: Rewiring Your Hypnotic Rhythm

> *"Any impulse of thought that the mind repeats*
> *over and over through habit*
> *forms an organized rhythm."*
>
> Napoleon Hill

Our repeated thoughts and habits become the rhythms by which we live. Unfortunately many of our rhythms consist of negative thought patterns deeply embedded in our unconscious. Many of us are stuck in these harmful, debilitating beliefs. The power of Neuro–Linguistic Programming (NLP) crushes beliefs that don't serve you. It frees you from harmful thought patterns.

My coach, and longtime friend Donald Currie is an NLP practitioner, naturo–therapist and hypnosis instructor. He has outlined the power of NLP for this chapter and explains how to engage it.

Regular meditation is a habit that successful people practice. The majority of high achievers meditate on their dreams and desires; understanding the power of calming their minds through controlled breaths. Did you know your lungs are the only organ you can control at will? Because most people are shallow breathers, they don't use their full lung capacity and therefore never use their full lung capacity. With practice, you will learn to control your breathing and access another secret of the super successful – the *stomach brain*.

In this section we will access your internal guidance system and intuition. This is often referred to in Eastern cultures as Kundalini, an ever–present spiritual energy that bestows the state of yoga, or divine union, upon the seeker of truth (you). Kundalini is a powerful practice to introduce into your life.

## Hypnotic Rhythm

Once you decide to become more successful, your mind becomes the most powerful tool for achieving the goal. With your mind, anything and everything is possible. Your mind either works for you or against you, based on your programming. This programming is often referred to as *hypnotic rhythm.*

Hypnotic rhythms are automatic and repeated thoughts, patterns and behaviors that your subconscious mind acts upon. They are ingrained, occurring outside of your conscious awareness.

Hypnotic rhythm was first explained by Napoleon Hill in his book *Outwitting the Devil*:

*"You will better understand me if I compare it to the method by which one learns to play music. At first the notes are memorized in the mind. Then they are related to one another through melody and rhythm. By repetition the melody and rhythm become fixed in the mind. Observe how relentlessly the musician must repeat a tune before he masters it. Through repetition the musical notes blend and then you have music. Any impulse of thought that the mind repeats over and over through habit forms an organized rhythm. Undesirable habits can be broken. They must be broken before they assume the proportions of rhythm. Any thought or physical movement that is repeated over and over through the principle of habit finally reaches the proportion of rhythm. Then the habit cannot be broken because nature takes it over and makes it permanent."[4]*

The subconscious mind is always learning. It was present when you learned how to ride a bike, tie a shoe, and brush your teeth. Through repeated practice these eventually became second nature. In the same manner, every time you receive a repeated verbal suggestion from the world outside, or a repeated self–reflective thought from within you, these thoughts and suggestions, through reinforcement, eventually became your hypnotic rhythms.

---

4    Napoleon Hill, Outwitting the Devil (New York: Sterling, 2011).

It is essential that you are aware of your hypnotic rhythms; they will define your outcome in life. They are the reason people succeed or fail in their endeavors. By changing your subconscious programming and hypnotic rhythms, you can begin to attract new and wonderful changes into your life.

So how do you change your hypnotic rhythms? First, it's important to understand exactly how your mind works. This will enable you to change thinking, create new hypnotic rhythms, and shape the neurons within your physical brain.

Let's explore the mind and its two very distinct parts, the conscious and subconscious.

Your mind can be compared to an iceberg. The conscious mind is the tip of the iceberg – only 10 percent is visible. The conscious mind allows you to be aware, to use logic and analyze, and to make judgments as to what's right and wrong. It is only responsible for 10 percent of your daily activity. Above the surface, the iceberg appears relatively small, but below the surface of the water, much is happening with the 90 percent of the iceberg that remains unseen.

The subconscious is this large part of the iceberg that sits below the surface – 90 percent of the mind. The subconscious is a complex system. It remembers everything you have ever heard, felt, seen or experienced in your life. It is responsible for all of your body processes: your breathing, heart rate, blood pressure, blinking, and digestion. It is also the storehouse of experiences, learning, instinct, self–preservation functions, emotions and feelings. All habitual and behavioral programming is stored within the subconscious mind, including your belief systems.

The subconscious mind moves within a fixed system of programming. It reacts automatically to life situations, basing these responses on your past behaviors. Because it works subconsciously, you are usually unaware of the responses taking place. Around 90 percent of your responses are subconscious. Even when you believe you are acting consciously, much of the time your subconscious is actually making the decision for you. Your subconscious is formulating your response about one-third of a second before you act. It has the ability to process around forty billion bits of information per second. This makes its potential far greater than the conscious mind.

Your hypnotic rhythms are stored within your subconscious mind, and these rhythms began before you were even born. The subconscious mind is aware even in utero, absorbing and learning every feeling, perception and sound. This is why babies respond to the voices of their parents from the moment they're born, they recognize them from the past nine months. As you grew, your subconscious mind continued developing your hypnotic rhythms based on the experiences you had, the things you were told and your own internal perceptions and thoughts of experiences. Suggestions from your parents, friends, teachers, and even the media have most likely played a very large role in the formation of your hypnotic rhythms.

When you decide to make a change, say to eat healthier, exercise, or stop smoking, you are making the choice to change with your conscious mind. This is what can make change difficult, because you are making the decision to change within your *conscious* mind, while the programming that supports the behavior is within the *subconscious* mind.

If you want to change any aspect of yourself, including how you relate to life and the world around you, you must learn how to tap into your mind. NLP and hypnosis can be very beneficial tools, allowing you to make changes deep within your subconscious. Working in these deep levels of your mind enables you to release feelings, change belief systems, realign yourself with new patterns of habit and behavior, and develop new thinking. It's a catalyst to make the changes you want. It allows you to change your hypnotic rhythms by eliminating the ones that are harmful to your success. And by cultivating new, empowering hypnotic rhythms, you will achieve success in every area of your life.

## NLP and Hypnosis

Hypnosis has gotten a bad rap over the years with most people equating it to a Vegas magic act. Hypnosis is actually a laser–like state of concentrated focus. You enter into a hypnotic state when watching a movie or driving a car. The average person enters hypnosis three to four times per hour (this state is also called daydreaming or zoning out). It is a naturally occurring, altered state of consciousness where the subconscious mind becomes more open to positive suggestion and instruction. Many geniuses of the past used forms of self–hypnosis to access higher levels of cognitive functioning. Einstein used to describe "the dreamlike trance into which people like myself fall when immersed in scientific work."[5]

Hypnotic rhythms are easier to change when someone is in a state of hypnosis because there is greater access to the deeper levels of the mind. In hypnosis, suggestions are more readily accepted by the subconscious mind, and through repetition and reinforcement, the subconscious responds to this new programming.

Positive suggestion, also known as direct suggestion, is a technique that allows new suggestions to form in the subconscious mind. For example, if you think, "There is no way I could ever speak in front of a large group of people." A new, positive suggestion might be, "I am fully capable of speaking in front of others. When I am in front of a group of people, I feel calm, relaxed, confident, and speak with ease." As we established earlier in this chapter, the mind learns through repetition and reinforcement. The more someone hears positive suggestions and instructions, the more these thoughts will become ingrained.

Two additional techniques that allow you to change your hypnotic rhythms are auto–suggestion and thought stopping:

---

5    Roger Highfield, The Private Lives of Albert Einstein (New York: St. Martin's Griffin, 1994).

- *Auto–suggestion* is the process of repeating a positive affirmation, suggestion, or instruction. With repeated practice, the positive affirmation or suggestion eventually becomes permanent.

- *Thought stopping* is a process that allows you to recognize when there is a negative, undesirable thought, feeling, or perception present. It then helps you let go of the thought and replace it with a positive one. When this is practiced regularly, the positive thought becomes automatic and overrides the negative thought.

Both of these techniques give you greater control over your thoughts, and with this newfound control, you will begin to refocus and redirect your thoughts in new ways. This will lead to greater focus, heightened creativity, increased motivation, higher levels of cognitive functioning and increased relaxation.

### Telling Your Story

Schedule some time each day to do the exercises that allow you to change your hypnotic rhythms. Consistency is key. Random practice sessions usually fail to bring your desired result. Begin taking ten minutes each day to practice the positive programming exercises.

At first these techniques will feel challenging and unfamiliar. Some days you may doubt if they will work at all. But as the days and weeks go on, your positive programming will begin to emerge. "Practice makes perfect." By practicing, you will feel more comfortable and familiar with these tools until they eventually become second nature. With regular practice, these techniques will be used automatically as you go about your daily activities. Your mind will automatically replace negative thoughts with positive thoughts.

After repetitive practice of these exercises, perhaps in only a few weeks, you'll experience a paradigm shift – a tipping point where all your new hypnotic rhythms programmed into your subconscious mind begin to work. Over time these thoughts will become more and more prevalent and after a few months, it will be as though a full transformation has taken place.

Do you procrastinate? Try a new mantra of "Do it now, get it down." You'll amaze yourself with how quickly your approach changes. "Let me do this now" will be your automatic response when faced with tasks.

Remember that change takes time. Be gentle with yourself and realize that this is a process. Practicing these exercises is like building a house brick by brick, and creating new thinking is building a new foundation. Be patient and have faith, your positive change will come.

## Living Among the Stars

It is no secret that Hollywood A–listers often use hypnosis as a means of self–improvement. Many well–known people have benefited from the power of hypnosis, meditation, and trance states. Matt Damon, Ellen DeGeneres, Brad Pitt, and Charlize Theron all successfully stopped smoking with the use of hypnosis.[6] Tiger Woods has used hypnosis ever since he was young. He currently uses a mixture of hypnosis, NLP, meditation, and visualization to improve concentration, mental focus, and hand–eye coordination. He has often stated how important hypnosis has been to his success.[7]

When Kevin Costner was filming *Water World*, he developed a terrible seasickness that prevented him from continuing on set. He flew a hypnotist to Hawaii, where they were filming, and after treatment he was able to resume filming. It saved the production of the movie.[8]

---

6  www.nationalhypnotherapysociety.org/about/news/charlize-theron-uses-hypnotherapy-to-give-up-smoking/
7  www.nationalhypnotherapysociety.org/about/news/charlize-theron-uses-hypnotherapy-to-give-up-smoking/
8  www.meridianpeakhypnosis.com/kevin-costner-hypnosis-movie-set-filming/

Bill Gates and Mark Zuckerberg regularly use meditation to recharge their brains, as did Steve Jobs. Much of their success can be attributed to the fact that they regularly clear their minds and restructure their thoughts.

## Steps to a Better You

Your brain is made up of billions of cells called neurons that use electricity to communicate with one another. The activity of the brain is commonly referred to as a brainwave pattern.

There are five main brainwave patterns:

1. Beta – *an energized state of focus and concentration*
2. Alpha – *a state of creativity and relaxation*
3. Theta – *a state of deep relaxation and meditation*
4. Gamma – *a state of optimal brain functioning and increased mental ability*
5. Delta – *a sleep state*

We are going to focus on Gamma brainwave exercises; they help you experience greater mental clarity, increased cognitive functioning, improved memory and a coherent focus.

## Benefits You May Experience from this Exercise

- *Increased Relaxation*
- *Reduced stress levels*
- *Heightened mental and emotional clarity*
- *Raised GABA, HGH, serotonin, DHEA, melatonin and endorphin levels*
- *Improved memory and learning*
- *Greater feelings of well–being*
- *Reduced pain*
- *Stronger focus and concentration*
- *More energy*
- *Increased IQ*

On your journey to success, you will have four audio programs to help you create new hypnotic rhythms. This section will provide you with detailed steps for implementing these into your own life.

It takes **21 days** to develop new thinking within the subconscious mind. Practice each week's exercise for at least seven days before moving on to the next. Once you have completed all four weeks, you can then revisit any program you choose on a daily basis.

- Week 1 – *The Manifestation Machine*
- Week 2 – *Thought Stopping*
- Week 3 – *Auto–suggestion*
- Week 4 – *Gamma Brainwave Program*

Remember that consistency is the key to success! Show up for yourself each and every day in order to create new hypnotic rhythms and embrace positive change.

## Week 1 – The Manifestation Machine

*Listen to* **Success Meditation 12–A**, *the Manifestation Machine, every day for the next seven days. It will serve as an introduction and foundation for the next four weeks.*

Everything you have experienced and learned in your life has brought you to the place you are right now. In the field of hypnosis, a formula called the Manifestation Machine is used to understand how hypnotic rhythms are created within the subconscious mind. It is the exact same formula that can help you undo old hypnotic rhythms and create new ones.

The suggestions you received from the outside world when you were a child affected your thinking, especially in terms of your identity and overall life view. These suggestions became the foundation of your hypnotic rhythms. For example, some of the suggestions you may have heard are "you need to work hard to make money" or "Money is scarce and hard to come by."

Things said by others imprint themselves deeply within the subconscious. Words become ingrained in the brain, creating neuro–pathways. With reinforcement and repetition, suggestions become the basis of our thinking. Eventually these thinking patterns occur automatically without any conscious effort.

Likewise, your thinking, through repetition and reinforcement, becomes your belief system, even though it may be far from the truth. Your belief system affects both your actions and your behaviors.

Someone who is told they are stupid may begin to believe it and not bother studying for the test. Because they believe they aren't smart, they believe they will fail regardless of whether they study or not. Someone who is told they are overweight may go ahead and eat that extra donut because they already believe they are heavy. They eat to fulfill that belief. These are the negative results of such suggestions.

Your actions and behaviors have defined your outcome in life as either positive or negative, and have led to positive or negative results. Sometimes a person who is told they are overweight might become very conscious of what they eat and decide to make healthy food choices. Eventually they lose weight as a result. This would be a positive result of such a suggestion.

### Week 2 – Thought Stopping

*Listen to* **Success Meditation 12–B** *daily for the next seven days.*

Positive and negative thoughts are like leaves traveling down a stream, they endlessly float. Some leaves are green. These are the fresh leaves that have just fallen from the tree and are still alive. Then there are the old dead leaves that are brown and withered. Let the green leaves represent your positive thoughts, and the dead leaves act as your negative thoughts.

Research by the National Science foundation concluded that the average person thinks about 12,000 thoughts a day, while deep thinkers reach 50,000.[9] It is estimated that *70 percent of those thoughts are negative.*[10] If you're having a bad day, this percentage can be even higher. Since much of your thinking is automatic, this statistic proves that thinking these negative thoughts is instinctive.

The more a trail is used, the more prominent it becomes. If you were to drive off the road into a forest, it would be difficult because you would be attempting to create a new path. All the vegetation would make it difficult to form a new path. But through repeated journeys this new path would eventually form. This is just like your way of thinking. Negative thoughts are the trail that has been traveled many times; it's familiar and comfortable. When you think more positively, you are taking the road less traveled and forging new paths

Another way to look at negative thoughts is to think of your mind as a garden. Negative thoughts are like weeds, while positive thoughts are like flowers. Don't water the weeds in your garden – pull them out. Once the weeds are gone, you can tend to the flowers and give them the attention and care they need to thrive.

Are you aware of what you are thinking each and every second of the day? And are you aware that your thoughts are creating your reality?

*Mindfulness* and *awareness* are the first steps to transforming negative thinking into positive thinking. Once you are made aware of your negative thoughts, you can change them into positive ones.

The principle of thought stopping allows for greater control of your thinking. When you become aware of a thought that's undesirable, you stop it and replace it with a desirable positive thought. It will become automatic as you continue to practice.

---

9    www.hvacprofitboosters.com/what-are-you-thinking-part-deux-by-charlie-greer.php#.Vfh6rp1Viko
10    www.psychologytoday.com/blog/sapient-nature/201310/how-negative-is-your-mental-chatter

It is beneficial to think positive thoughts, but research has proven that people who are optimistic have stronger immune systems than those with negative outlooks.[11] A positive outlook helps you to better cope with stress, remain more relaxed, and have an improved mood on a day–to–day basis.

In the following exercise, you will have the opportunity to put thought stopping to work by answering questions and evaluating your responses. Learning this powerful technique will enable you to have greater control of your thoughts, allowing you to pull out the weeds and plant roses in the garden of your mind.

### Week 3 – Auto–Suggestion

*For the next seven days, listen to* **Success Meditation 12–C** *and practice the auto–suggestion exercise outlined below.*

Auto–suggestion is another simple and effective tool to redirect old hypnotic rhythms and develop new ones. The purpose of auto–suggestion is to reprogram your subconscious thought repetition.

The auto–suggestion process is:

1.   Place your hands on your lap, with one hand on each leg.

2.   Repeat your goal out loud, while pressing down on your legs with each finger until you have reached a repetition of ten.

Example: Say, *"On July 1, 2017, I am successfully self–employed,"* as you press into your leg with your thumb. Restate the same phrase as you press into your leg with your index finger. Repeat the process with each finger until ten repetitions have been made.

Auto–suggestion can be done while stuck in traffic, while on the subway, or anywhere else where you are unable to go into a state of hypnosis.

---

11   www.pursuit-of-happiness.org/science-of-happiness/posi-tive-thinking/

The mind learns through repetition, so with repeated use of auto–suggestion your goals are further embedded into the subconscious. The more you practice auto–suggestion, the more effective it will become.

## Week 4 – Gamma Brainwave Program

*Listen to* **Success Meditation 12–D** *every day for the next seven days. This will help you to absorb all the information you have learned in the previous three exercises.*

Binaural beats can assist in increasing the level of gamma wave activity in brain wave patterns. They are specific frequencies used to shift brainwave activity into altered states of consciousness. Clinical studies have shown they are a safe and effective way to influence brainwave patterns. They've been proven to reduce stress, heighten creativity, induce sleep, and help with learning.

Binaural beats must be listened to using good–quality stereo headphones. Each ear receives a slightly different tone and frequency. A third tone is created by the brain, and is essentially the combination of both tones. This third tone is tuned to one of the five different brainwave states. The listener hears it as a wavering tone. The brain follows this tone in a phenomenon called frequency following response. As a result, the mind enters a state of consciousness tuned to the binaural tone.

A phenomenon called hemispheric synchronization also occurs while listening to binaural beats. This causes the left and right brain to start working together in harmony. Some of the most brilliant minds in history had a high degree of whole–brain synchronization, leading them to incredible accomplishments.

## Putting It All Together

This chapter has educated you on the myriad powers of NLP and hypnosis. You have learned about positive auto–suggestion and thought–stopping techniques, both of which will allow you to take control of your thoughts and take action toward the achievement of your DGAs.

**Playbook Exercise 12:**

1.  *Tracking Positive and Negative Suggestions*

    Take your journal and track two beliefs: one that manifests negative results and one that manifests positive results.

    The self–evaluation and reflection questions will empower you to gain needed clarity and insight into the inner workings of your mind. The self–hypnosis tools and exercises will empower you to release old patterns of thought, behavior, and feeling that are no longer serving you. These tools will enable you to realign your subconscious mind with positive thoughts, behaviors, habits, and beliefs.

2.  *Self–Reflection Exercise – Thought Stopping*

    -   Do you recognize any negative hypnotic rhythms in your life?

    -   Which ones do you most frequently think about?

    -   How often do you have these thoughts?

    -   If you could change these thoughts to something more positive, what would those thoughts be?

    With this new, positive thinking, how would it change:

    -   The way you think?

    -   The way you feel?

    -   The way you behave?

3.  *Self–Reflection Questions for Auto–Suggestion*

    -   How many times did you practice auto–suggestion today?

    -   How did you feel *before* you practiced auto–suggestion?

    -   How did you feel *after* you practiced auto–suggestion?

- Did you notice any changes in your behavior?

- Did you notice any changes in your thoughts?

- Did you notice any changes in the way you felt?

- Did you find yourself taking any new actions?

- Do you feel that you need to increase the amount of auto–suggestion you are doing? If so, how many times per day?

## Success Meditation #12: – Four Part Manifestation Machine

There are four meditations referenced in Chapter 12, they may be found here:

www.ChristopherCumby.com/SuccessMeditation

**JOURNAL NOTES:**

**JOURNAL NOTES:**

_____

_____

_____

_____

_____

_____

_____

_____

_____

_____

_____

_____

_____

_____

_____

_____

_____

# 13 The Ultimate Application: Building Your Success Playbook

The lessons from the *Success Playbook* have the power to change your life. These important principles, these keys to creating a successful life, work, but only if you invest the time to learn, apply, and take action in your life. Please note that I am only the messenger and did not create all the information – I simply assimilated and synthesized it for you so that it will be easy to understand and use.

Your life, as you know it, has already changed. As you apply the lessons you've just learned, your life will become what you want it to be. But only if you believe. Do not underestimate the power of faith.

You now have the number one tool for creating success in your life – a journal, your own *Success Playbook*.

Before I wrap up this book, I want to share with you my inspiration for writing this book. A business collapse forced me to take stock and evaluate what wasn't working. I realized, as I took notes, wrote in my journal and began to take action that in evaluating what didn't work, I discovered what *did* work. The pillars of success were created.

I knew I wanted to share this knowledge with my children, and my handwritten *Success Playbook* was to be their guide. It was a simple journal with my personal insight, but it lit a light within me. I was ready to take action and realize my dream of becoming an author.

Not knowing how it was going to happen, or even how to get started, an email from my mentor, Brian Tracy, came across my desk shortly thereafter, titled: *"How to Write a Book and Become a Published Author."* Brian's program arrived in the mail, filled with CDs, workbooks, manuals and educational resources. Then it sat on my desk for two years.

One day, after completing a meditation with an intention of *getting started*, I did. I envisioned myself as a published author, sharing my wisdom with others and at that moment I knew I would complete this book.

Armed with technology, and inspired while exercising, I walked each day and imagined I was walking as far as I could write. The next day, I would do the same and be able to write a little more. I walked approximately 1.9 million steps while writing my book, using a Nike Fuel Band to monitor my activity. I used Google Docs, on my phone, to dictate most of the book while walking. I removed the excuse of not having enough time and made time by combining a love (being outdoors, walking) with a want (being an author).

This is a major lesson – don't allow excuses to get in your way. We're all busy. We are all crunched for time. But the takeaway is this: If you want something, as Nike says, "Just do it!"

In this book, we have learned to take the pillars of success and apply them to your own life. You've gained insight into what it takes to become an accurate thinker. You've learned how to make decisions effectively and to create better habits. You understand the power of your journal. You've been introduced to the *Who A.R.E. You?* principle. You know how to enhance your goal–setting abilities through dream building. You understand what *focus* can manifest once you engage it. And you know that *you* are the creator of your life and everything in it.

You can create anything you dream about, set goals for and want to have. A strong will and a dedication to discovering yourself, through journaling, will allow you to start living the life you want. Let's review your roadmap to success using the techniques and exercises we've learned in your *Success Playbook*.

## The Ultimate Application

In the first four chapters, you learned the four pillars, your fundamental steps, to building your ideal life. Let's examine them.

## 1. Be Careful Who You Listen To

Take inventory of the people you'd like to provide insight into your own journey to success. Who has what you want? Who has a similar story to yours, or one you're looking to create? Whose biography can you read? What documentary can you watch? How can you gain this insight or inspiration to help support your own DGAs?

## 2. Keep Learning

Be a student of life. Perfect the art of discernment. This process will give you a clear understanding of the four stages we covered: *unconscious incompetence, conscious incompetence, conscious competence,* and *unconscious competence.* When you put your knowledge to work, directing it toward your chief aim (purpose) in life, there will be no stopping the law of attraction. Your vibration/frequency will reflect that positive energy and push you toward your DGAs. The right people, places, and things will find you.

## 3. Accept Change (Be the Change to See the Change)

Learning to accept change can be daunting. In fact, it is the number one reason why most people don't pursue their DGAs. Change can be uncomfortable, it's not what you're accustomed to and that scares many of us. But when you accept change as positive force, as an adventure and not a punishment, you'll start to see exciting changes all around you.

Review Playbook Exercise 3. What areas of your life would you like to see changed? What are you looking for? Why do you want it? What feeling will this change give you? Why do you want to feel that way? What is missing from your life now? Have your answers now that you've progressed further through this book? Good! You change daily, your DGAs will, too.

### 4. Know Why You Want Something (Make the Why Big Enough)

> "When you know who you are, you'll know where you are going."
>
> Christopher Cumby

It's not just about achieving your DGAs, it's also about why you want them. The universe provides you with the right people, places, events and circumstances to put your DGAs into action. Pay attention to what appears. The universe works in mysterious ways, some experiences may not make sense at first sight. Trust that you are being guided. Stay positive, even in seemingly negative situations, and you will excel in your journey toward your dreams.

What is your big WHY? Why do you want what you want? Read over *Playbook Exercise 4*. Know it. Recite it. Repeat it. Own it.

These pillars are your foundation. Once you master these, your life will change course. These are simple yet effective truths and by mastering them, you'll have the confidence to face whatever comes your way. You will inevitably encounter challenges, but the key is to never give up.

### The Golden Rule

You've changed your life already just by reading this book. The techniques I've shared with you are designed so you can jump–start your life and go after whatever you want.

One of the most important aspects of creating and attracting positive outcomes in your life is the Golden Rule: Treat others the way you'd like to be treated. This proverb tends to get overlooked in today's noisy world. As our world evolves, my hope is that people will remember its significance and apply it to their personal interactions.

Napoleon Hill stresses its importance, saying:

> "There is an eternal law through the operation of which we reap that which we sow. When you select the rule of conduct by which you guide yourself in your transactions with others, you will be fair, and just, very likely, if you know you are setting into motion, by that selection, a power that will run its course for wealth or woe in the lives of others, returning, finally, to help or hinder, according to its nature."

This rule really defines the power of the universe. When you practice this and really apply it to your life, you will see how we all are connected. There is no separation, and even encountering an unfavorable situation not slanted in your favor, you will have the choice to react in a positive and constructive manner.

Live by this rule. Practice it in every situation you encounter in life. Because when it comes to the wheel of success, what goes around comes around.

Journaling will unlock so many doors for you. You've already begun the process with Playbook Exercises, here are some reminders as you continue to expand and fine–tune your DGAs through journaling.

### Building Your Success Playbook: The Do's

#### DO be honest with yourself
*Don't fool yourself*

This will be the first chapter of your own *Success Playbook*. Be open and honest with yourself. Confront the challenges in your life. Be in control.

> "Honesty is the first chapter in the book of wisdom."
>
> Thomas Jefferson

**DO commit to this process**

*You are powerful.*

When you make the decision to pursue a different life, it will bring to you the people, places, events and circumstances needed to support this choice. You have the power to make this happen. Unleash it.

**DO keep going no matter what**

*Don't let your dreams be taken from you*

Had J.K. Rowling given up, the magic of Harry Potter would never exist. Publishers rejected her repeatedly. She was a struggling single mom whose dreams have resulted in global book sales of more than 400 million copies over $15 billion dollars from books, movies, toys and now theme parks. Let her life be a lesson to you – never give up!

> "I have seen many storms in my life. Most storms have caught me by surprise, so I had to learn very quickly to look further and understand that I am not capable of controlling the weather, to exercise the art of patience and to respect the fury of nature."
>
> Paulo Coelho

**DO set your intentions in the affirmative**

*You have to believe that you can achieve*

When setting your intentions, writing your goals, and thinking about their outcomes, you must do so in the affirmative, meaning you are in agreement with them. An example: "I am in the process of attracting all that I need to be, do, and have in order to live my ideal lifestyle."

**DO be patient**

*Don't lose sight of the end goal*

Your timeline and the universe's timeline for you may not always be in sync. Be patient and stay focused on what you want.

## DO have confidence

*Start today, get experience, you'll continue to improve*

Confidence comes from knowledge, expand your mind by reading inspiring books and surrounding yourself with the right influencers.

> "Don't wait until everything is just right. It will never be perfect. There will always be challenges, obstacles, and less than perfect conditions. So what? Get started now. With each step you take, you will grow stronger and stronger, more and more skilled, more and more self-confident, and more and more successful."
>
> Mark Victor Hansen

## DO be persistent

*No excuses – go after what you want*

Helen Keller was deaf, blind and mute, but with the help of her teacher, Anne Sullivan, Keller thrived. She learned to read, write and communicate, writing her biography at age 22 and becoming an inspiration to the world.

## DO set yourself up to win

*Don't put too much pressure on yourself, it will weaken you*

Practice being positive. Build your success by breaking your day down into smaller chunks. This is your priority list; keep it to six priorities or less each day. Schedule the hardest tasks first, tackle them early in the morning to ensure your focus is clear and your energy is high. You will be amazed at the progress you make when you break things down into manageable pieces. As a bonus, the completion will give you an incredible feeling of accomplishment, giving you a winning and strengthening your resolve to achieve your DGAs.

> "But failure has to be an option in art and in exploration – because it's a leap of faith.
> And no important endeavor that required innovation was done without risk. You have to be willing to take those risks..."
>
> James Cameron

## DO have faith, take risks, and get out of your comfort zone
*Don't underestimate the power of faith*

You must have faith that you will attain the life you want. It takes an element of risk, moving outside your comfort zone to pursue your dream down the road less traveled. Trust yourself.

## DO practice the 5 C's

Be confident about where you are going. Commit to your DGAs. Get creative and design the loftiest, wildest DGAs you can imagine. Find clarity in your thoughts, words and actions. Be credible – do what you say you're going to do.

## DO practice mindful meditation
*Take time for your thoughts*

Mindful meditation, like focus, can manifest powerful outcomes. Silence, solitude, thoughtfulness and deep, cleansing breaths unleash your power within. This is why meditation is necessary in life.

> "The thing about meditation is: You become more and more you."
>
> David Lynch

## DO exercise your mind and body
*Negative thoughts and a neglected body keep you from living the life you really want.*

A fit mind and body will help you accomplish what you set your mind on. Feeling good while pursuing your happiness is a sure way to reach your goals faster. Having a sound body and mind should be a primary focus in your life.

> "The mind and body are like parallel universes. Anything that happens in the mental universe must leave tracks in the physical."
>
> Deepak Chopra

## DO find mentors or coaches to assist you

*You don't have to go it alone*

Having a mentor/coach is critical to achieving your goals. They help you see your blind spots. They will inspire you. They'll give you the right motivation when you need it most. They will keep you accountable and offer feedback on your progress as you seek your success.

> "A mentor empowers a person to see a possible future, and believes that it can be obtained."
>
> Shawn Hitchcock

## DO create the self–image that fits your desired outcome

*Be the person you aspire to be*

Self–image is one of the most important aspects of creation. People don't have what they want because they don't allow themselves to have it; their self–image isn't aligned with the frequency of what they want. The words you speak have power. Illuminate that power with the vibration and frequency of your words. Be mindful of your words because this will align your self–image with what you want.

## The End of the Road, the Beginning of Your Journey

It is my hope that this book has provided you with the foundation necessary for a life filled with happiness and success. When you focus your attention on mastering these fundamentals, your life will change. For the better!

> "The person we believe
> ourselves to be
> will always act
> in a manner consistent
> with our self–image."
>
> Brian Tracy

The appendix includes a list of other incredible books to assist you on your journey. I believe they will resonate with you, as they have with me. I am also confident that this recommended reading will reinforce the strategies and techniques we've learned throughout the *Success Playbook*.

My hope is that the *Success Playbook* has earned a permanent place on your shelf, in your mind, and in your heart. Move forward in your life knowing that with a dream, the right tools, and the right people, you too will live a life worth living.

Your journal is your number one tool for achieving the success you've always dreamed about. Applying the lessons you've learned within this book will take you there.

Ultimately I created a life worth living. I am proud to tell you that my life is filled with happiness and abundance and I continue to find success both personally and professionally.

Cheers to *your* success!

## APPENDIX: RECOMMENDED READING

### Manifesting

*Think and Grow Rich* by Napoleon Hill (original version)

*The Law of Attraction* by Esther Hicks and Jerry Hicks

*The Science of Getting Rich* by Wallace D. Wattles

*The Law of Success in Sixteen Lessons* by Napoleon Hill

*Conversations with God* by Neale Donald Walsch

*The Strangest Secret* by Earl Nightingale

*You Were Born Rich* by Bob Proctor

### Feel Good Now

*You Can Heal Yourself* by Louise Hay

*I Can See Clearly Now* by Dr. Wayne W. Dyer

*The Seven Spiritual Laws of Success* by Deepak Chopra

### Life Skills

*Self–Reliance* by Ralph Waldo Emerson

*The Psychology of Achievement* by Brian Tracy

*Awaken the Giant Within* by Tony Robbins

*See You at the Top* by Zig Ziglar

*Abundance* by Peter H. Diamandis and Steven Kotler

*Bold* by Peter H. Diamandis and Steven Kotler

# ACKNOWLEDGMENTS

This book took shape in my mind years ago, as I found myself asking:

*Why am I failing?*
*Why is this happening to me?*

These two questions pushed me to gain a deeper understanding of my direction and myself. *The Success Playbook* that you hold in your hands was written for a reason – to help others realize their potential in their own lives.

I am dedicating this book to my wife, Julie. She inspires and encourages me and I honestly could not have achieved this dream without her incredible support. It is also dedicated to my four children – they motivate me, spark my creativity and bring me such joy. My family is my *WHY*.

I am giving some special thanks to the people who taught me to be stronger and more loving every day.

Thank you, Rick F., for the invite to Author 101 University. It opened my eyes to the possibility of becoming an author and for that I will always be grateful.

A special thanks to KT, who has been an amazing mentor and awakened inside me the soul of my existence. KT's training has changed who I am and allowed me to reach a more heightened consciousness.

Thank you to my close friend, John D., for being a part of my crazy mastermind.

Thank you to Brett Toskan and Gary Green (*Greener*) for allowing me to share your stories.

To my cousin, and best friend, Trevor, who encourages me to keep moving forward and just *pay the 20*.

To my friend Gary K.: Thank you, I treasure our friendship.

Thank you to my friend Carmine, who was creative and instrumental in my business with design, ideas, and knowledge.

Thank you Miladinka Milic "Meella" for your creative design collaboration.

To my longtime friend Jim T. for being there for me during one of the biggest life lessons I had to learn. Thank you for being empathetic and compassionate friend.

To Brennan M., who mentored me in my early entrepreneurship and allowed me to find my dream: You showed me that an ideal life is possible. Thank you.

Thanks to Darren P., who brought out the competitive salesperson in me and helped shape my path. You taught me that even the sky has no limit when you have a dream.

To two of my best friends, Nick M. and Kyle P., thank you for your continued support and loyalty. You are both gentlemen and true friends.

Many thanks to Publishizer and our supporters, what an incredible community that I'm so proud to be a part of.

Thank you to my students, clients, customers, followers, fans, and supporters for everything you do.

I also want to thank the people who have taught me the lessons of adversity. Without these people I would not have known who I really am and what I was able to accomplish.

A huge thank you to my parents who taught me to be kind and care about others in every aspect of life.

Many thanks to Donald Currie for contributing to this book and teaching me to find my inner voice and myself.

And a very special thank you to my writing coach, Justin S. Justin, you are a class act and it brings me great pleasure to call you my friend.

I am very happy to bring you *The Success Playbook*. It is the culmination of my own journey and I am hopeful it will help you along yours.

Thank you, dear reader, for allowing me to share in your journey. I am so excited to see what your futures hold!

Sincerely,

Christopher L. Cumby

Author, The Success Playbook

## VERY SPECIAL THANKS

Matthew Basta, Kristin Boehm, Marika Cederberg, Michael Coopersmith, Danny Cumby, Lloyd Cumby, Riley Dayne, Mark DeAngelis, Jessica Devenny, Jeff Dooley, Lorraine Dooley, George Dudas, Julie Eason, Rosana Filipe, Valerie Georgantas, Jean–Philippe Giguere, Jerry Gladstone, Mike Greenly, Maureen Griffiths, Daniel Hall, Warren Haughie, Peter Hwang, Michael Kerwin, Estella Lau, Cathy Mahon, David Marleau, Willy Martin, Nancy McKenzie, Karlton Meadows, Sylvie Methot, Sean Moffatt, Nick Morabito, Eric Nelson, Darryl Oake, Trevor Oake, Joshua Roy, Kay Sanders, Carley Simandl, Bradlee Snow, Robert Suter, Xavier Torres, Brett Toskan, Guy Vincent, John William Waller, David White, Steven White

# ABOUT THE AUTHOR

For more than 15 years, Chris has been coaching and advising clients on both business strategies and personal development. What began as a position in sales and marketing took on a broader scope of business advisement when he identified a disconnect that occurred amongst his clients. Seeing business growth as an extension of personal growth, Chris saw that his clients achieved greater success in their professional  lives when they also focused on positive personal development. With this realization, Chris saw the opportunity to branch out and offer consultancy services that benefit the person, not simply the organization.

In 2003 Chris founded Integrity Marketing Inc., a direct sales consulting platform focused on creating new opportunities and new revenue streams for his American and Canadian clients. Integrity Marketing has consistently helped its clients achieve broader market shares, increased revenues and greater profits.

The *Success Playbook* brand, dedicated to personal enrichment, was developed to provide consulting services to his clients. Capitalizing on this success, Chris has authored a book on his approach to personal development that allows him to help more people in their search for self–fulfillment.

Chris's core expertise lies in working closely with people to help design, implement and execute their personal development and sales strategies. Chris has been instrumental in the positive growth of each client with whom he has worked, and helped to contribute to their overall success.

# YOUR SUCCESS PLAYBOOK

CPSIA information can be obtained
at www.ICGtesting.com
Printed in the USA
BVHW07s1337240918
528340BV00029B/1259/P